AUTHORS

Carlo Cucut was born in Nole (TO) in 1955. He has cultivated a passion for history since he was a boy and over the years has deepened this interest by devoting himself to historical research. He has published articles in the magazines, "History of the 20th Century," "Stories & Battles," "Milites," and "Ritterkreuz." In the publishing field, he has published several volumes for Marvia Editions: "Penne Nere on the Eastern Border. History of the Alpine Regiment "Tagliamento" 1943-1945," winner of the De Cia Prize; "Attilio Viziano. Memories of a War Correspondent"; "Armed Forces of the CSR on the Eastern Front"; "Armed Forces of the CSR on the Western Front"; "Armed Forces of the CSR on the Gothic Line"; "Alpini in the City of Rijeka 1944-1945." For the Gruppo Modellistico Trentino he published "Armed Forces of the CSR 1943-1945. Ground Forces."

Paolo Crippa, (April 23, 1978) has cultivated a passion for Italian History, especially World War II, since his high school days. His research focuses mainly in the field of military history and in particular on armored units from the 1930s until the end of World War II. In 2006 he published his first volume, "I Reparti Corazzati della Repubblica Sociale Italiana 1943/1945," the first organic research completed and published in Italy on the subject, which was followed by "Duecento Volti della R.S.I." (2007), "A Year with the 27th Legnano Artillery Regiment" (2011) and "The Counter Guerrilla Units of the R.S.I." (2020). He has to his credit more than forty articles for the journals Milites, Historica Nuova, SGM - Second World War, Batailes & Blindes, Ritterkreuz, War Fronts, Mezzi Armorzzati, Storia & Battaglie, Umago Viva, La Martinella, and Storia del Novecento, both as an author and in collaboration with other researchers, and has carried out collaborations and consultations for other authors in the writing of historical-uniformological texts. Since 2019 he has been collaborating with Luca Cristini Editore in the creation of the series "Witness to War" and since 2020 he has been its Director. With Mattioli 1885 he published "Italy 43-45. The circumstantial armored vehicles of the Civil War" (2014), "The Italian armored vehicles of the Civil War 1943-1945" (2015) and "Italy 43-45. The Means of the Cobelligerent Units" (2018).

PUBLISHING'S NOTES

None of unpublished images or text of our book may be reproduced in any format without the expressed written permission of Luca Cristini Editore (already Soldiershop.com) when not indicate as marked with license creative commons 3.0 or 4.0. Luca Cristini Editore has made every reasonable effort to locate, contact and acknowledge rights holders and to correctly apply terms and conditions to Content.
Every effort has been made to trace the copyright of all the photographs. If there are unintentional omissions, please contact the publisher in writing at: info@soldiershop.com, who will correct all subsequent editions.
Our trademark: Luca Cristini Editore©, and the names of our series & brand: Soldiershop, Witness to war, Museum book, Bookmoon, Soldiers&Weapons, Battlefield, War in colour, Historical Biographies, Darwin's view, Fabula, Altrastoria, Italia Storica Ebook, Witness To History, Soldiers, Weapons & Uniforms, Storia etc. are herein © by Luca Cristini Editore.

LICENSES COMMONS

This book may utilize part of material marked with license creative commons 3.0 or 4.0 (CC BY 4.0), (CC BY-ND 4.0), (CC BY-SA 4.0) or (CC0 1.0). We give appropriate attribution credit and indicate if change were made in the acknowledgments field. Our WTW books series utilize only fonts licensed under the SIL Open Font License or other free use license.

For a complete list of Soldiershop titles please contact Luca Cristini Editore on our website: www.soldiershop.com or www.cristinieditore.com. E-mail: info@soldiershop.com

Titolo: **BULGARIAN ARMOURED DIVISIONS** Code.: **WTW-046 EN** By Carlo Cucut and Paolo Crippa
ISBN code: 9788893279963 first edition July 2023
Language: English; size: 177,8 x 254mm; Cover & Art Design: Luca S. Cristini

WITNESS TO WAR (SOLDIERSHOP) is a trademark of Luca Cristini Editore, via Orio, 35/4 - 24050 Zanica (BG) ITALY.

WITNESS TO WAR

BULGARIAN ARMOURED DIVISIONS

FROM THE 1ST ARMOURED COMPANY TO DISBANDMENT OF THE BRONIRANA BRIGADE 1935 - 1947

PHOTOS & IMAGES FROM WORLD WARTIME ARCHIVES

CARLO CUCUT - PAOLO CRIPPA

BOOKS TO COLLECT

CONTENTS

The kingdom of Bulgaria .... Pag. 5

The establishment of the first armoured divisions .... Pag. 7

The armoured regiment .... Pag. 25

The Bronirana Brigada .... Pag. 37

The coup d'état .... Pag. 51

    The first phase of the patriotic war .... Pag. 52

    The second phase of the patriotic war .... Pag. 78

The post-war period and the disbanding of the Bronirana Brigada .... Pag. 87

Camouflage, insignia, registration number .... Pag. 93

Bibliography .... Pag. 98

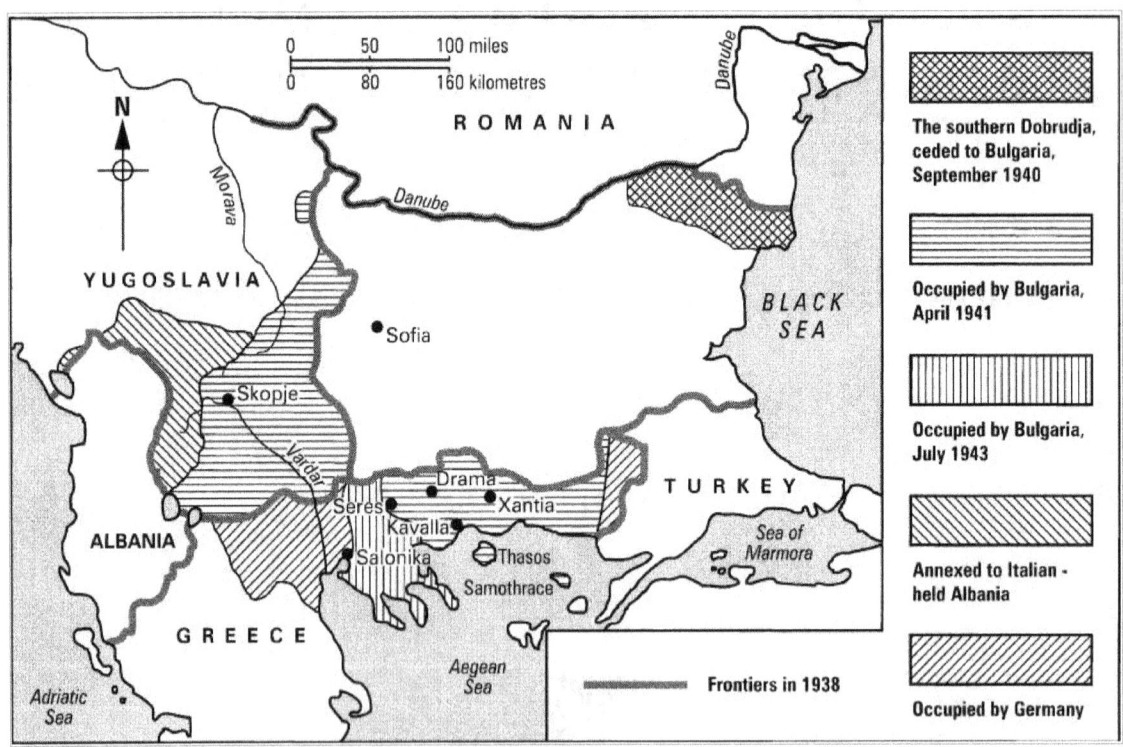

▲ Map representing Bulgaria with the territories annexed or occupied during World War II.

THE KINGDOM OF BULGARIA

The Kingdom of Bulgaria was established on 5 October 1908 by Prince Ferdinand I, who, taking advantage of the ongoing international tensions, declared the end of Ottoman sovereignty over the Principality of Bulgaria and formalised the annexation of the province of East Rumelia, which had already been under Bulgarian control since 1885. Elevating the Principality of Bulgaria to a Kingdom, Prince Ferdinand I was crowned Tsar on 5 October in the Church of the Forty Martyrs in Veliko Tărnovo.

In 1912 and 1913 the Kingdom of Bulgaria was involved in two Balkan wars: the first, allied with Serbia and Greece, against Turkey, the second alone against Serbia, Greece and Romania. The two conflicts cost heavy human losses and considerable territorial changes. In fact, at the end of the first Balkan War, the Kingdom of Bulgaria acquired numerous territories, which it then lost after the conclusion of the second.

The political consequences of the Balkan Wars for the Bulgarians were a strong resentment towards Russia and the Western powers, which remained neutral during the conflicts and left the young Kingdom isolated. The consequence of this attitude led the Kingdom of Bulgaria to ally itself with Germany and the Austro-Hungarian Empire, even though this alliance meant becoming a de facto ally of the Turks, the historical enemy of the Bulgarians. Since Serbia, Greece and Romania, allies of France and the United Kingdom, possessed some territories lost during the Balkan wars that it intended to recover, when World War I broke out and Germany promised to restore the borders of the Treaty of San Stefano, the Kingdom of Bulgaria declared war on Serbia in October 1915. As a direct consequence of this declaration of war, the United Kingdom, France and Italy also declared war on the Kingdom of Bulgaria.

Despite numerous victories won against the Romanians and Serbs, the Russian Revolution in 1917 led to the spread of sentiments against the monarchy, both in civil society and in the army, creating the conditions for its downfall. Then, in September 1918, when the Serbian, British, French and Greek armies broke through the Macedonian front, Tsar Ferdinand was forced to ask for peace. If the war was over, albeit with a defeat, what was worrying was the risk of a revolution, which forced Tsar Ferdinand to abdicate in favour of his son Boris III.

With the Treaty of Neuilly of 27 November 1919, the defeated Kingdom of Bulgaria at the end of the First World War, in addition to the territorial losses and war damages to be paid to the victorious nations, had to undergo a severe downsizing of its armed forces as well as the limitation of the possession of numerous items of equipment, which is why the modernisation of the Bulgarian army was postponed for several years. The army was considerably weakened, with a reduced number of personnel and few modern weapons at its disposal, as well as the impossibility of acquiring those means, e.g. armoured vehicles, that would, a few decades later, monopolise conflicts.

In June 1923, a popular uprising broke out, organised by the Communist Party, which was bloodily suppressed by the army and the Macedonian Internal Revolutionary Organisation, a right-wing movement in favour of resuming the war to reconquer Macedonia, with the approval of Tsar Boris III. In May 1934, a new coup d'état was suppressed and, in April 1935, Boris III took power directly by appointing a puppet prime minister.

Tsar Boris III banned all opposition parties, forged alliances with Germany and Italy and, in 1938, signed the Balkan Pact, by which good relations were restored with Yugoslavia and Greece, although territorial issues remained unresolved.

With the Treaty of Craiova of 7 September 1940, imposed by Nazi Germany, Bulgaria regained possession of Southern Dobruja, ceded by Romania. On 1 March 1941, Bulgaria joined the Tripartite Pact, becoming an ally of Germany, the Japanese Empire and the Kingdom of Italy. In preparation for the invasion of the Kingdom of Greece and the Kingdom of Yugoslavia, Bulgaria allowed German troops to enter its territory. Following the defeat of Yugoslavia and Greece, Bulgaria occupied Greek Thrace and most of Macedonia.

Subsequently, the Kingdom of Bulgaria declared war on Great Britain and the United States but not on the Soviet Union, despite continuous German pressure. In August 1943, Tsar Boris III died suddenly after a trip to Germany[1]. Power was then assumed by a regency group headed by Prince Kirill and his mother Queen Jeanne of Savoy, as the heir, Prince Simeon II, was only 6 years old.

In early 1944, Soviet troops were rapidly advancing towards the Bulgarian borders and the Allies carried out some disastrous bombing raids on the capital Sofia and other locations. In August, the Kingdom of Bulgaria, whose emissaries had engaged in secret negotiations with the Allies to get out of the war, announced the cessation of hostilities and demanded that German troops leave Bulgaria. At the same time, their troops were rapidly withdrawn from Greece and Yugoslavia. In the first days of September 1944, the Soviets crossed the northern border and began their invasion of Bulgaria. The government, in an attempt to avoid a Soviet invasion, declared war on Germany.

The Bulgarian army then began fighting alongside the Soviet troops against the former German allies, contributing to the liberation of Yugoslavia, Hungary and Austria.

▲ Tsar Boris III during an official ceremony together with senior army officers in the second half of the 1930s.

---

1   For years it was suspected that he had been poisoned by the Germans, but this was never officially proven.

THE ESTABLISHMENT OF THE FIRST ARMOURED DIVISIONS

During the First World War, the Bulgarian army used neither armoured nor armoured vehicles; only in 1917 was a group of officers sent to Germany to see and study captured Allied tanks. During the battle on the Dobruzhansky front in Romania, an Austin-Putilov armoured car was captured from Russian troops, but there is no knowledge of its use by the Bulgarians and its demise. Due to restrictions under the peace treaty clauses, the difficult economic situation and political instability, which lasted from the early post-war years until the 1930s, the first Bulgarian tanks were only purchased in 1934. The Ministry of War (Ministerstvo na vojnata) decided to purchase 14 CV33[2] fast tanks produced by Ansaldo from Italy. In addition to the supply of the tanks, the contract also provided for the supply of 100 Pavesi P4 Mod. 30 artillery tractors, with payment deferred over 6/8 years. The CV33s were delivered to the port of Varna in early 1935.

The Bulgarian tank differed from the Italian one in terms of its different armament, in fact, instead of the two 6.5 mm Fiat Mod. 14 aviation-type machine guns, there was an 8 mm Schwarzlose machine gun. All Ansaldos were sent to the 2nd Automotive Battalion in Sofia, where they formed the 1st Tank Company, becoming a unit of the 1st Engineer Regiment. Command of the Company was assumed by Major Boris Tenev Slavov, the other officers were Lieutenants Todor Stefanov Ivanov, Angel Stefanov Nerezov and Stojan Stojanov. The total staff consisted of four officers and 86 non-commissioned officers, graduates and troops.

In the course of 1936, the 2nd Tank Company was formed, under the command of Major Slavov, with a staff of 167 men but, at the time, no tanks.

On 4 September 1936, the Bulgarian War Ministry signed a contract with the British company Vickers-Armstrong for the purchase of eight Vickers Mark E tanks[3] equipped with a 47-mm cannon and a Vickers .303 machine gun. The Vickers tanks arrived in Bulgaria in early 1938 and were delivered to 2nd Tank Company, which formed two platoons each equipped with four tanks. During the year, the 2nd Tank Company participated in joint exercises with the motorised infantry and motorised artillery.

On 1 January 1939, with 1st and 2nd Company, the 1st Armoured Battalion was formed, under the command of Major Todor Ivanov Popov, while 1st Company was under the command of Lieutenant Ivan Ivanov Gjumbabov and 2nd of Lieutenant Todor Stefanov Ivanov.

The 1st Armoured Battalion consisted of:

- Headquarters
- 1st Company: 14 Ansaldo
- 2nd Company: 8 Vickers
- Repair Workshop

with a staff of 173 men

In the manoeuvres that took place in 1939 near the town of Popovo, both 1st and 2nd Tank Company participated. The 1st Company was then deployed along the southern border at Kolarovo and Kharmanlijsko, and the 2nd along the northern border near Polski Trmbesh and Rusensko, supporting the 5th 'Danube' Infantry Division.

---

2   The CV33 fast tanks in Bulgaria were named 'Ansaldo-Fiat'.
3   The Vickers Mark E tanks in Bulgaria were named 'Vickers'.

In February 1939, Bulgarian officers attended a demonstration of Czechoslovak light tanks and were favourably impressed by some of the vehicles. Negotiations were then held with Czechoslovakia for the purchase of 50 Tančík Tank vzor 33 and 40 Lehký Tank vzor 35 (LT-35) light tanks. Due to the German occupation of Czechoslovakia in March 1939, the negotiations were interrupted, but in August, the Bulgarian government managed to reach an agreement with Germany for the supply of a large amount of war material. The purchased material included 26 LT vz. light tanks. 35[4], which, upon their arrival in February 1940, enabled the formation of the 3rd Armoured Company, under the command of Captain Alexander Ivanov Bosilkov.

The Armoured Battalion, now consisting of three companies, from 10 July 1940 was deployed in south-east Bulgaria on the border with Turkey, near the towns of Lozen and Ljubimec, where it was engaged in manoeuvres. The 1st Company was instead deployed in September 1940 during the occupation of southern Dobruja, obtained from Romania following the implementation of the Treaty of Craiova.

Recognising the quality of the LT vz. 35 tanks, an additional 40 tanks were requested in March 1940, but the Germans offered the same number of LT vz. 38 tanks, but these were refused by the Bulgarian Army as they were considered too light. The Germans then offered 10 Škoda T-11 tanks, a different version of the LT vz. 35 built for the Afghan army and never delivered, which differed mainly from the LT vz. 35 by the new A7 cannon that replaced the original A3 vz. 34, also 37 mm. The German offer was accepted and between November 1940 and February 1941, the 10 T-11 tanks[5] were delivered.

Following Bulgaria's accession to the Tripartite Pact, the Germans in April 1941 delivered 40 French pre-war Renault R35 light tanks[6] at a favourable price, also providing instructors for the training of Bulgarian tank drivers. With these new tanks, the 4th Tank Company was established.

---

4   The Lehký Tank vzor 35-LT vz. 35 in Bulgaria were named 'Lek Tank Škoda Š-35' - Лек танк Skoda, but were commonly called Škoda.
5   The Škoda T-11 tanks in Bulgaria were named 'T-11'.
6   The Renault R-35 tanks in Bulgaria were named 'Reno'.

▲ A Russian Austin armoured car captured by the Bulgarians in November 1916 in Romania and used for a short period.

▼ Ansaldo fast tanks B60001 and B60002, belonging to the 1st Tank Company, pictured at the end of an event with two children as crew.

▲ An Ansaldo fast tank, belonging to the 1st Tank Company, camouflaged with bushes, engaged in exercises in the early 1930s. Note the dark green camouflage on the uniform light green.

▼ Ansaldo fast tanks, belonging to the 1st Tank Company, during manoeuvres in the mid-1930s.

▲ Officers, soldiers and tank drivers pose for a photograph on an Ansaldo fast carriage after the occupation of southern Dobruja in September 1940.

▼ Ansaldo fast tanks, belonging to the 1st Tank Company, parade in the town of Dobrich in September 1940 after the occupation of southern Dobruja.

▲ Ansaldo fast tanks, belonging to the 1st Tank Company, engaged during the occupation of southern Dobruja in September 1940.

▼ The 1st Tank Company, equipped with CV33 fast tanks, deployed in the mid-1930s before participating in an exercise.

▲ Ansaldo fast tank, belonging to the 1st Tank Company, during an exercise in the 1930s. The three-colour camouflage is clearly visible.

▼ A Vickers Mark E tank, belonging to the 2nd Company, proceeds masked with shrubs and plants during summer manoeuvres, second half of the 1930s.

▲ A Vickers Mark E tank, with its crew, during training. Note that the 47 mm cannon has been removed.

▼ A Vickers Mark E tank, belonging to 2nd Company, during crew training in the second half of the 1930s.

▲ A Vickers Mk. E tank in the barracks before the 1941 manoeuvres, an Ansaldo fast tank can be seen on the left.

▼ Tankers and officers in front of the Vickers Mark E tank, B60021, belonging to 3rd Company in 1941.

▲ A Vickers Mk. E tank, belonging to the 2nd Company of the 1st Armoured Battalion, engaged in winter manoeuvres in 1940.

▼ A Vickers Mk. E tank of the 2nd Company filmed inside the barracks, note the three-coloured camouflage.

▲ A Vickers Mk. E tank of the 2nd Company during training in the late 1930s. The three-colour camouflage is clearly visible.
▼ Tsar Boris III engaged in summer manoeuvres in 1941 in command of a Škoda tank.

▲ The 3rd Armoured Company, equipped with Škoda tanks, deployed at the end of the manoeuvres. The first three tanks: B60057, B60056 and B60055, are Škoda T11s, the version armed with the A7 gun.

▼ Škoda T-11 tank engaged in summer manoeuvres in 1941, some R35 tanks can be seen behind the vehicle.

▲ Škoda tank engaged in manoeuvres from 7-21 September 1941.

▼ A Škoda tank inside the barracks in Sofia in the late 1930s.

▲ The Renault R35 'Reno' tank, B60202, belonging to the 2nd Armoured Battalion, engaged in summer manoeuvres in 1941.

▼ Freshly delivered Renault R35 'Reno' tanks, together with Škoda LT vz. 35 of the 1st Battalion, in April 1941.

▲ An R35 'Reno' tank, belonging to the 2nd Armoured Battalion, photographed in the barracks.

▼ Bulgarian soldiers around a Renault NC27 tank captured from the Yugoslavs in 1941.

▲ An Ansaldo fast tank filmed in the fields of southern Dobruja in September 1940.

▼ A photograph, unfortunately of poor quality, of an Ansaldo fast carriage during a presentation of the vehicle to the military authorities in the mid-1930s.

▲ Vickers Mark E tank B60022 engaged in fire manoeuvres in the mid-1930s.

▼ A Vickers Mk. E tank parades on 6 May 1940 in Sofia during the parade for St. George's Day, the feast day of the Bulgarian army, followed by a formation of Škoda LT vz. 35.

▲ Ansaldo fast tanks, belonging to the 1st Company of the 1st Armoured Battalion, during manoeuvres in 1937.

▼ Three Vickers Mk. E tanks, B60015 - B60016 - B60017, belonging to the 2nd Company of the 1st Armoured Battalion, during the Great Imperial Manoeuvres of September 1941.

THE ARMOURED REGIMENT

In April 1941, the 1st Armoured Battalion participated in joint exercises with the 16. Panzer-Division of the Wehrmacht in the vicinity of the town of Pazardžik, in the presence of Tsar Boris III who, impressed by the operational capabilities of the German units, gave the order to strengthen the armoured units by establishing a new Armoured Regiment. Following the partial mobilisation, declared in the spring of 1941, and with the arrival of the R35 tanks, the Bulgarian armed forces were able to establish the 2nd Armoured Battalion, consisting of 4th, 5th and 6th Company. On 25 June 1941, the two Armoured Battalions formed the 1st Armoured Regiment (1st Bronirana polk). The Regiment was quartered in the barracks of the 1st Cavalry Regiment and organically depended directly on the Army General Staff. The command of the 1st Armoured Regiment was assumed by Major Todor Ivanov Popov.

The 1st Armoured Regiment consisted of:

- Headquarters
- Exploring Company
- 1st Armoured Battalion
    - 1st Company: 3 platoons
    - 2nd Company: 3 platoons
    - 3rd Company: 3 platoons
- 2nd Armoured Battalion
    - 4th Company: 3 platoons
    - 5th Company: 3 platoons
    - 6th Company: 3 platoons
- Repair workshop
- Motorised Infantry Group
- Motorised Artillery Group
- Various services

The tanks in service were: 14 Ansaldo, 8 Vickers, 26 Škoda, 10 T-11 and 40 R35, as well as 24 3-tonne Opel Blitz trucks, 18 BMW R-35 motorbikes and 2 Praga motorbikes.

At the end of July, the Armoured Regiment, which was actually a small Brigade, was transferred to a new facility at Camp Knjas Simeon, located approximately 10 km west of Sofia.

The tank crews were not as satisfied with the Škoda tanks as they were with the R35s, which, among other things, were delivered with many missing or faulty components, as well as being second-hand and worn out. The new commander, Lieutenant Colonel Geno K. Genov, complained about the serious shortage of radio equipment, as well as doubting that the problems with the R35 tanks were due to sabotage in France where the tanks had been shipped.

As of 15 August, the 1st Armoured Regiment/Brigade had a staff of 1,802 men, young and motivated personnel, unfortunately with little training due to the impossibility, up to that point, of conducting fire manoeuvres with tanks and artillery.

At the end of October, the two armoured battalions of the 1st Regiment, together with other Bulgarian units, were sent to Nova Zagora from where, during training, they moved by road to Yambol, in central-eastern Bulgaria, to participate in manoeuvres. During this transfer, many R35 tanks belonging to the three companies of the 2nd Battalion had to stop, due to mechanical problems and the poor road conditions caused by heavy rain and mud. The 2nd Battalion was practically put out of service due to the mechanical failures suffered by its R35s!

It went much better for the companies of the 1st Battalion, both the 1st and the 2nd, equipped with Škodas, and the 3rd, with Vickers, carried out the road transfer without major problems and participated in manoeuvres with the other units.

The end of 1941 saw the 1st Armoured Regiment/Brigade essentially unchanged since its establishment, the insufficient number of tanks, the absence of armoured cars and the shortage of trucks/special vehicles/cars had prevented the planned increase in personnel. The only supply of new material during the year was bridge material for the Engineer Company.

In March 1942, changes were made to the organisation of the units within the 1st Armoured Regiment, which, as a result of a change in the allocation of available means, took on the following composition[7]:

- Brigade Headquarters: 3 Škodas (one with radio)
- Headquarters Armoured Regiment: 2 Škodas (one with radio)
- 1st Armoured Battalion
    - Staff: 2 Škodas (one with radio)
    - 1st Company: 17 Škoda (4 with radio)
    - 2nd Company: 17 Škoda (4 with radio)
    - 3rd Company: 8 Vickers and 5 Ansaldo
- 2nd Armoured Battalion
    - Command: 1 R35 (with radio) and 3 Ansaldo
    - 1st Company: 13 R35 (all without radios)
    - 2nd Company: 13 R35 (all without radio)
    - 3rd Company: 13 R35 (all without radio)
- Reconnaissance Platoon: 5 Ansaldo

The 3rd Company of the 1st Battalion, equipped with Vickers tanks, was mainly assigned the task of anti-tank fighting. The Regiment/Brigade was also assigned a new motorised anti-aircraft battery, equipped with 15 20 cm machine guns and 15 light machine guns.

On 19 March 1942, a platoon of Škodas and a platoon of R35s carried out shooting exercises, the Škodas firing the 37 mm cannon while the R35s fired machine guns. The targets were placed at a distance of between 200 and 400 and the results were flattering, satisfying the Bulgarian and German observers. At the end of the exercises, it was noted that the firing training of the crews was considered to be good, while for manoeuvres there were still many shortcomings, demonstrating a considerable lack of skill.

The Germans, who considered the Regiment to be a small Brigade, while appreciating the good progress made through continuous training, did not fail to point out some serious deficiencies. The main shortcomings were related to the R35 tank in the 2nd Armoured Battalion. In addition to the lack of radio equipment, it was the low speed that was the greatest limitation compared to the Škoda tanks, an obvious constraint that would have prevented the unified use of the armoured regiment.

The German advisors therefore recommended replacing the R35s with new Škodas or medium tanks equipped with 75 mm cannons, as well as purchasing modern armoured cars for the scouting unit, light mortars for the infantry and more bridge equipment for the Engineer Company.

From 29 to 31 May, a number of exercises were carried out near Sofia, with the aim of testing whether some of the problems that had emerged in previous manoeuvres had been overcome. If the armoured units showed some improvement, the scouting unit again demonstrated its inefficiency.

---

7   The numbers of Škoda tanks in the table do not correspond to the actual tank allocation, in fact, against a total of 36 Škoda LT-35 and T-11 tanks delivered by the Germans, the personnel tables provided for a total of 41 tanks. It is probable that the personnel tables were as planned but were never implemented due to the shortage of vehicles.

The need to be supported by a German officer from the Panzer divisions to act as a full-time adviser and trainer became even more apparent. On 11 July 1942, Lieutenant Colonel Freiherr von Bülow assumed this position.

The main problem Von Bülow faced was to improve the combat tactics of the tank units and the coordination between tanks, infantry and artillery. At the end of August, not even a month after his arrival, the major manoeuvres took place near Pernik with the presence of numerous units of the Bulgarian armed forces. During these manoeuvres, the[8] Brigade displayed numerous shortcomings, from poor camouflage to advanced grouping that did not conform to the rules, from uncoordinated forward movement with the infantry to the risk of encirclement due to the lack of infantry and artillery support.

Further manoeuvres were carried out between 3 and 4 September and between 14 and 20 October, the latter at the training camp in the vicinity of Nova Zagora, in both exercises the Brigade showed considerable improvement.

At the end of 1942, the Brigade numbered 3,809 men, including officers, non-commissioned officers, graduates and troops.

On 1 January 1943, Staff Colonel Heinrich Gäde replaced Lieutenant-Colonel Freiherr von Bülow as military adviser to the Brigade.

As a result of the arms agreement between Germany and Turkey, Bulgaria's historical enemy, signed towards the end of 1942, the '*Barbara*' plan between the OKW and the Bulgarian Minister of War was drawn up on 5 January 1943, which envisaged equipping 10 Infantry Divisions, one Cavalry Division and two Armoured Brigades with modern German weapons.

Bulgaria therefore requested from Germany the supply of: 90 medium tanks, 140 light tanks, 55 StuG III assault guns, 84 light and 54 heavy armoured cars, 186 troop transport half-tracks, to equip the two Armoured Brigades. Among the required tanks, in addition to the Pz.Kpfw. IV, there were 25 Pz.Kpfw. I for training and 10 Pz.Kpfw. III. The request was rejected by the Germans who, in February, declared that they were only prepared to deliver 12 Pz.Kpfw. IV, 20 StuG III and 20 light armoured cars.

The number of armoured vehicles envisaged by the Germans was in line with the plan proposed by the OKW, which envisaged an armoured regiment consisting of only one tank battalion in each of the two armoured brigades to be formed, a plan that was, however, rejected by the Bulgarians who argued for two tank battalions in each regiment.

While discussions continued on how many and which vehicles to deliver, Colonel Gäde, with the aim of optimising the operation of the units with the available and soon-to-be-delivered vehicles, recommended that the Škoda tanks should remain in service in the Armoured Regiment, while the R35s should no longer be part of it and be used to form special units to support the infantry. He considered that the R35s were too slow, unable to manoeuvre in coordination with the other tanks and had inadequate armament for the tasks assigned to the new armoured regiment.

Instead, the Vickers tanks were to be used as armoured observation vehicles for the Brigade's artillery batteries, while the Ansaldo fast tanks were to be used as armoured ambulances and as ammunition carriers.

The Gäde proposal envisaged the following structure for the Armoured Regiment:
- Regimental Headquarters
- 1st Armoured Battalion
- 1st Medium tank companies
- 2nd Medium tank company
- 3rd Light Tank Company

---

8   Although not officially, given the presence of infantry, artillery and tanks, the unit was now considered a Brigade.

Within each company there were two Ansaldo fast tanks, one to support the repair department and the other as an ambulance for the medical NCO.

With the transfer of the means planned by the Germans, the tanks in service in the Regiment would have been:

- 12 Pz.Kpfw. IV[9]
- 20 StuG III[10]
- 36 Škoda/T-11
- 14 Ansaldo

Colonel Gäde, on 29 January 1943, also recommended the establishment of two or three batteries of assault cannons to accompany the infantry, both to strengthen offensive capabilities and because of the great impact their presence would have on troop morale. A request was then made by the Bulgarian General Staff for the total supply of 55 StuG III assault guns instead of the 20 allocated in the initial German plan.

The training of personnel, intended to train the crews for the new vehicles, accelerated in the spring of 1943, when 41 officers and 37 non-commissioned officers were sent to the German Armoured School in Wünsdorf, and, at the German Combat School established in Niš in Serbia, a special course was started on 12 April for Bulgarian tank drivers destined for Pz.Kpfw. IV and StuG III.

The Bulgarian War Ministry had in the meantime rejected the organisation of the Armoured Regiment proposed by Colonel Gäde, asking instead to form the 2nd Armoured Battalion using R35s together with 5 StuG IIIs, while the 1st Battalion would operate with Škodas and Pz.Kpfw. IV, and with the remaining 15 StuG IIIs, assault gun batteries would be formed under the operational command of the Brigade Artillery Regiment.

The Bulgarian proposal was partially accepted by the OKW, which, after renegotiating the agreement on the supply of armoured vehicles, in late March and early April decided to increase the number of Pz.Kpfw. IV to be supplied by increasing the quantity first from 12 to 43 vehicles and then to 91. With regard to assault guns, the Germans also decided to increase the number of StuG IIIs to be delivered, from the planned 20 to the requested 55 vehicles, specifying, however, that these vehicles were not to be placed within the Brigade's artillery regiment, but were to be placed in independent formations to support the infantry.

Between February and May 1943, the Germans delivered 14 modern medium tanks Pz.Kpfw. IV[11] and the first 15 StuG III Ausf.G assault guns, means destined to become the standard equipment of the Bulgarian armoured forces, which made it possible to allocate the more obsolete tanks to training and/or infantry support tasks in anti-partisan operations.

The first 5 StuG III Ausf. G were delivered in February, followed by a further 10 between March and April, the next 40 vehicles arrived in four monthly batches: 10 in batch 2 in May, 10 in batch 3 between June and July, 10 in batch 4 from August to September and the last 10 in batch 5 from the end of September to November, thus enabling Bulgaria to have all 55 StuG IIIs planned by the end of 1943[12].

---

9   The Pz.Kpfw. IV in Bulgaria were referred to as 'boyna kola Maybach T-IV' - бойна кола Maybach T-IV, where the T indicated that the vehicle was German, but the common designation was most often T-IV. In some cases it is referred to as 'Majbakh T-IV'.
10   The StuG III assault guns in Bulgaria were named SO-75 ('samokhodno orudie' - self-propelled gun) or StuG 40, although some sources refer to them as 'Majbakh T-III'.
11   3 Bulgarian Pz.Kpfw. IV Bulgarians were detached to the German combat school in Niš, remaining there until Bulgaria's declaration of war on Germany in September 1944, when they were captured by the Germans and re-employed by their units.
12   The delivery of the 55 StuG IIIs in 5 lots as described in reality did not take place, as only 25 vehicles were delivered during 1943, with the remaining 30 arriving between January and February 1944.

On 10 June 1943, the 1st SAO - shturmovo artileriĭsko otdelenie (Assault Artillery Detachment) was established in Sofia, which remained in the capital until September 1944, when it was sent to fight in Yugoslavia. On 10 September, the 2nd SAO was established, also in Sofia, which, in November, was transferred to the town of Haskovo while in April 1944 it was sent to the village of Uzundzhovo and then moved to Plovdiv. The 1st SAO was incorporated into the 1st Army and the 2nd SAO into the 2nd Army.

Each SAO was structured on:

- Headquarters
- Battery Headquarters: 2 StuG III
- 1st Battery - 1 StuG III battery command + 3 Platoons each with 2 StuG IIIs
- 2nd Battery - 1 StuG III battery command + 3 Platoons each with 2 StuG IIIs
- 3rd Battery - 1 StuG III battery command + 3 Platoons each with 2 StuG IIIs

In total, each SAO had 25 StuG III[13].

In place of the 25 Pz.Kpfw I training tanks and 10 Pz.Kpfw III tanks that the Bulgarian War Ministry had requested, the Germans, after initially refusing their delivery, negotiated a new agreement under which 10 Pz.Kpfw 38(t) in place of the Pz.Kpfw III, while 19 Hotchkiss H39 light tanks and 6 SOMUA S35 French pre-war tanks were proposed for the Pz.Kpfw I, which were no longer in production. The French tanks were rejected by Bulgaria, because of the bad experience with the R35s, but the Germans were adamant and did not change the materials they had identified and arranged for the Hotchkiss and SOMUA to be delivered. To mitigate the strong grievances of the Bulgarians, 13 Sd.Kfz. 222 and 7 Sd.Kfz. 223.

On 20 May 1943, the Germans delivered the 10 Pz.Kpfw 38(t)[14] as agreed. These were vehicles from the Ausf A, B, E, F and G series under repair at the ČKD factory, all of which were assigned to the 9th Company.

At the combat school in Niš, on 19 May 1943, the first course for Bulgarian crews destined for Pz.Kpfw. IV. Of the 14 tanks delivered by the Germans at the school, 3 remained available for the training of the other crews in Niš, while the other 11, with their respective crews, returned to Bulgaria and were divided among the four Tank Companies and used for training, pending the delivery of the other batches of Pz.Kpfw. IV.

Despite the arrival of the new tanks and the specific training at the German schools of tank drivers destined for the new vehicles, which had improved the quality of the Armoured Regiment, the Brigade continued to have a rather poor operational performance. For several months, Lieutenant Colonel Genov, the Brigade commander, complaining about the lack of petrol, personnel on leave, bad weather and other excuses, slowed down the training programmes established by the Germans. Faced with this uncooperative attitude, Colonel Gäde repeatedly complained to the Bulgarian War Minister, trying to solve the problem once and for all, but unfortunately his complaints had no effect.

The lack of training was so evident that, during the manoeuvres carried out in late August 1943 north of Sofia by both the Brigade and the assault cannon detachment, the evaluation of all units was poor.

As of 3 September 1943, a total of 46 Pz.Kpfw. IV.

---

13   The five StuG IIIs not in service in the two SAOs remained with the German combat school in Niš and, in September 1944 when Bulgaria changed alliance, were reused by the Germanic units.
14   The Pz.Kpfw 38(t) tanks in Bulgaria were named 'boĭna kola Praga' - бойна кола Прага, but were commonly referred to as 'Praga'.

▲ A Vickers Mk. E tank engaged in military manoeuvres at Yambol in 1940.

▼ Vickers Mk. E tank, B60021, belonging to 10th Training Company, in the barracks at Malo Bucino on 20 July 1944.

▲ Vickers Mk. E tank, B60017, of 2nd Company, filmed inside the barracks.

▼ Officers of the 1st Armoured Regiment pose in front of a Škoda T-11 tank engaged in summer manoeuvres in 1941.

▲ Officers belonging to the HQ of the 1st Armoured Regiment pose in front of a Škoda T11 tank, B60052, during summer manoeuvres in Nova Zagora in 1942.

▼ A Škoda LT vz. 35 surrounded by tank drivers during summer exercises in the late 1930s.

▲ An R35 'Reno' Company, engaged in exercises in the autumn of 1941, stops along a road greeted by the local population.

▼ Tank, artillery and motorised infantry officers, belonging to the Armoured Regiment, during summer manoeuvres in Nova Zagora in 1942.

▲ R35 'Reno' tank column on the move during manoeuvres in 1941.

▲ The Vickers Mk. E tank, B60017, painted uniform dark green, in the barracks at Malo Bucino in 1943.

▲ R35 'Reno' tanks, belonging to the 2nd Armoured Battalion, during summer manoeuvres in 1941. The first tank is registered B60203.

▼ Tank officers, together with German advisers, receive instructions from the commander of the 1st Armoured Regiment before starting exercises in Nova Zagora in 1942.

THE BRONIRANA BRIGADA

On 1 October 1943, in implementation of Ministerial Order No. 375 issued by the Ministry of War on 29 September, the 1st Armoured Brigade of the Bulgarian Army was officially established: the Bronirana Brigada (Бронирана бригада). In practice, the Armoured Regiment was elevated to the level of an Armoured Brigade, as it was already considered by the Germans, by expanding, restructuring and reorganising the units currently serving in the Regiment.

In the Armoured Regiment, structured on three Tank Battalions each with two companies on Pz.Kpfw. IV and one on **Škoda**, the lack of German tanks in the 3rd Battalion was compensated for by distributing the crews between the Companies of the other two to enable the crews to be trained, until the new Pz.Kpfw. IV. Each medium tank company was to have a tabulated strength of 14 Pz.Kpfw. IV[15].

A Genius Battalion was also formed out of two Engineer Companies, implementing the original Company present, and a Bridge Company, while the Transmission Company was expanded to Battalion, although still being completed.

With the arrival of the new tanks, it was finally possible to remove the Renault R35s from the Brigade's equipment. The R35s were transferred to the town of Sliven, where they were used against the partisan movement that was taking hold in the area. Subsequently, a unit consisting of 10 R35s was assigned in support of the 29th Infantry Division, belonging to the Bulgarian Occupation Corps in Serbia, stationed in Vranje and engaged in the fight against Tito's partisans.

In November, first Major Kahl, and shortly afterwards Colonel von Jungenfeldt, took over as the Brigade's training advisor. It was thanks to the tenacious work of Colonel Jungenfeldt that the Bronirana Brigada assumed its operational readiness in 1944.

During 1943, a clear sign of wait-and-see attitude on the part of the population and the military emerged with greater intensity, the continuous defeats suffered on all fronts by the Axis and the increasingly pronounced pro-Russian sentiment, which had in truth never waned in the previous years, became more pronounced. Especially among the officers, this attitude was evident, which took the form of delaying training, postponing assigned tasks, and showing little cooperation with the German personnel seconded to the Brigade.

On 15 December 1943, the Germans drew up a report in which they listed the armoured vehicles provided by the Armoured Regiment in the Brigade:
- Armoured Regiment
- 1st Tank Battalion
    - 1st Company: 14 Pz.Kpfw. IV
    - 2nd Company: 14 Pz.Kpfw. IV
    - 3rd Company: 16 Škoda
- 2nd Tank Battalion
    - 4th Company: 14 Pz.Kpfw. IV
    - 5th Company: 14 Pz.Kpfw. IV
    - 6th Company: 16 Škoda
- 3rd Tank Battalion
    - 7th Company: waiting for tanks
    - 8th Company: waiting for tanks

---

15   According to some authors, the number of tanks in the company was 14 or 15, but this number would correspond to a much higher number of Pz.Kpfw. IV delivered by the Germans much higher than the number actually registered in Bulgaria. The number of 12 Pz.Kpfw. IV per Company, quoted in other texts, is the one that most closely corresponds to the total number of tanks that entered service.

- o 9th Company: 10 Škoda 'Praga'
- Exploring Battalion: 13 M-222 and 7 M-223

As of 31 December 1943, the Germans had delivered the following tanks to Bulgaria:
- 46 Pz.Kpfw. IV
- 25 StuG III
- 10 Pz.Kpfw 38(t)
- 13 Sd.Kfz. 222
- 7 Sd.Kfz. 223

Between January and February 1944, 30 StuG IIIs were delivered, thus completing the order of 55 vehicles stipulated in the agreements, and 42 Pz.Kpfw. IV, making a total of 88 vehicles.

With regard to the total number of Pz.Kpfw. IV actually delivered and entered into service in the Bulgarian armoured units, some clarifications must be made, as different authors gave different numbers, as well as the type of tank model, until the change of alliance, because then, as we shall see later, many Pz.Kpfw. IV of different models were delivered by the Soviets to replace the losses incurred.

The official request from the Bulgarian War Ministry was an order for 91 tanks, to be delivered by 1943, which was fulfilled by the Germans by the spring of 1944. According to one source, the Pz.Kpfw. IV ordered and delivered were 97 by 1943, while the actual deliveries were 46 as indicated by the Germans in their December 1943 report, all of the G model according to at least two sources, while others indicate G and H models.

The number of Pz.Kpfw. IV tanks that officially received a registration in Bulgaria were 87, plus the 88th that was accepted into service but did not receive a plate, plus the 3 that were left at the combat school in Niš and were not registered, making a total of 91 vehicles.

According to another source, the Pz.Kpfw. IV would be delivered in seven batches and the tanks would be assigned to the following departments:
- 1st lot delivered on 30 April 1943: 3 Pz.Kpfw. IV - Combat School in Niš
- 2nd lot delivered between 24 and 31 May 1943: 11 Pz.Kpfw. IV - assigned to the 4 Companies of the 1st and 2nd Battalion to continue training
- 3rd lot delivered between 11 and 20 June 1943: 15 Pz.Kpfw. IV - assigned to the 1st Battalion, 8 to the 1st company and 7 to the 2nd
- 4th batch delivered on 15 August 1943: 15 Pz.Kpfw. IV - assigned to 2nd Battalion, 11 to 4th Company and 4 to 5th
- 5th lot delivered between 11 and 20 September 1943: 15 Pz.Kpfw. IV - assigned 4 to 1st company, 3 to 2nd, 7 to 5th
- 6th lot delivered between 1 and 7 November 1943: 15 Pz.Kpfw. IV - assigned to 3rd Battalion, 8 to 7th company, 7 to 8th
- 7th batch delivered between 1 and 20 January 1944: 12 Pz.Kpfw. IV - assigned to 3rd Battalion, 6 to 7th company, 6 to 8th

In total, the armoured units of the Bulgarian Army would have had 86 Pz.Kpfw. IV of which 83 in the Bronirana Brigada and 3 at the German combat school in Niš.

German sources have always stated that they delivered a total of 88 Pz.Kpfw. IV to Bulgaria, which, in the report on the number of tanks in service on 1 June 1944, confirmed the number of 88 tanks received. It can therefore be stated that there were indeed 88 Pz.Kpfw. IV tanks delivered by the Germans to Bulgaria and used to arm the 3 Battalions serving in the Armoured Regiment of the Bronirana Brigada.

The capital of Bulgaria, Sofia, was heavily bombed by bombers belonging to the 15th Air Force on 10 January 1944, causing numerous casualties and heavy damage. As further air raids were possible, the Command ordered the transfer of the Bronirana Brigade away from the city area. The Headquarters and the Motorized Infantry Regiment were moved to Ihtiman, the Motorized Artillery Regiment to Vakarel, the Armoured Regiment to Novihan, while the Anti-tank, Reconnaissance and Engineer Battalions reached Samokov.

During the transfer to Novihan, 25 km from the capital, several Škoda and 'Praga' tanks were towed by Pz.Kpfw. IV. The bombing hit the barracks where the 1st SAO was stationed, resulting in the death of 7 soldiers, so it was ordered to move to Novoselze, 24 km from Sofia, where it was engaged in some operations against communist partisans. Instead, the 2nd SAO continued its training in Khaskovo, integrating new recruits.

In January and February 1944, 400 reservists arrived in the Bronirana Brigade, which helped to replenish the considerably undersized Armoured Regiment.

In February 1944, the Hotchkiss H39 and SOMUA S35 tanks were delivered, which, however, did not become part of the army, but were handed over to the Gendarmerie, who used them briefly in the fight against the partisan forces that had begun their activities in parts of Bulgaria.

During the winter and spring of 1944, the training of the Bronirana Brigada units continued under the supervision of German advisors. On 10 May, in application of a general decree issued by the Ministry of War to all units, the Bronirana Brigada was ordered to reach the staffing levels stipulated in the staffing tables and the full availability of vehicles in service within 5 days.

Colonel Gäde sent a detailed report on the situation regarding the Bronirana Brigade to the OKW on 1 June. In the report, it was specified that the staffing levels referred to the Armoured Regiment were at 70-75% with regard to the staffing tables, although it was emphasised that there was a serious shortage of technical personnel, while for the other divisions of the Brigade, they were at 80-90%. With regard to vehicles, it was reported that the availability of the Pz.Kpfw. IVs was 85 per cent, while the remaining vehicles were expected to be repaired within 14 days; for the Škodas, however, it was estimated that only 15 to 20 tanks could be repaired due to the shortage of spare parts. On the other hand, the availability of the motorised vehicles in the workforce was 85 to 90 per cent.

In his report, Colonel Gäde pointed out, for the umpteenth time, that the Brigade's training rating ranged from weak to acceptable, and that it would not be ready for action until the end of July. In addition, the organisation and equipment chart of the Bronirana Brigade provided for three Motorised Infantry Battalions and two Motorised Infantry Companies, but at the time there were only two of the former and one of the latter.

On 14 June, Colonel Gäde again recommended the immediate replacement of the Brigade commander, Colonel Genov, who was considered by the Germans to be unsuitable for command, as he did not possess the technical knowledge to command an armoured unit, showed little cooperation with the members of the German training mission, and had become commander of the Brigade, according to them, not because of his abilities, but because of his friendship with the late Tsar Boris III. Despite this umpteenth request for a replacement sent by the Germans, the War Ministry did not intervene and Colonel Genov remained in command of the Bronirana Brigade.

The Bronirana Brigada in July 1944 had the following structure:
- Brigade Headquarters
- Motorbike Platoon
- 1st Armoured Regiment
    - Headquarters
    - Armoured company: 13 Pz.Kpfw. IV
    - Maintenance Workshop

- o   Broadcast Platoon
- o   Engineer Platoon
- 1st Armoured Battalion
  - o   Headquarters: 1 Pz.Kpfw. IV
  - o   1st Company: 12 Pz.Kpfw. IV
  - o   2nd Company: 12 Pz.Kpfw. IV
  - o   3rd Company: 12 Škoda
- 2nd Armoured Battalion
  - o   Headquarters: 1 Pz.Kpfw. IV
  - o   4th Company: 12 Pz.Kpfw. IV
  - o   5th Company: 12 Pz.Kpfw. IV
  - o   6th Company: 12 Škoda
- 3rd Armoured Battalion
  - o   Headquarters: 1 Pz.Kpfw. IV
  - o   7th Company: 12 Pz.Kpfw. IV
  - o   8th Company: 12 Pz.Kpfw. IV
  - o   9th Company: 10 Škoda 'Praga'
- Reserve Tank Platoon: 12 Škodas
- 10th Training Company: 8 Vickers, 14? Ansaldo
- 11th Training Company: R35 (stationed in Sliven)
- 1st Motorised Infantry Regiment
  - o   Headquarters
  - o   Engineer Platoon
  - o   Motorbike Platoon
  - o   Broadcast Platoon
- 1st Motorised Fusilier Battalion
  - o   3 Rifle Companies
  - o   1 Accompanying Arms Company
- 2nd Motorised Rifle Battalion
  - o   3 Rifle Companies
  - o   1 Accompanying Arms Company
- 3rd Motorised Rifle Battalion
  - o   3 Rifle Companies
  - o   1 Accompanying Arms Company
- Reconnaissance Battalion
  - o   2 Motorcycle Companies
  - o   1 Armoured Car Company: 18 M-222 and M-223
- Genius Platoon
- Mortar Platoon
- Anti-tank platoon
- Motorised Maintenance Company
- Motorised Artillery Regiment
  - o   Headquarters
  - o   Battery observation platoon
  - o   Broadcast Platoon
- 1st Motorised Artillery Battalion
  - o   Transmission platoon

- - 3 Motorised batteries: 12 leFH 18 10.5 cm
- 2nd Motorised Artillery Battalion
  - Transmission platoon
  - 2 Motorised batteries: 8 sFH 18 15 cm
- Motorised anti-tank battalion
  - 2 light anti-tank companies: 18 PaK 38 5 cm
  - 1 Heavy anti-tank company: 6 PaK 40 7.5 cm
- Motorised anti-aircraft battalion
  - Light anti-aircraft battery: 12 FlaK 2 cm
  - Medium anti-aircraft battery: 9 FlaK 3.7 cm
  - Heavy anti-aircraft battery: 6 FlaK 8.8 cm
- Motorised Engineer Battalion
  - 2 Genius companies
- Transmission Battalion
- Various services

The total personnel of the Bronirana Brigada was 9,340 officers, non-commissioned officers, graduates and troops[16].

The total number of vehicles and weapons in service was: 140 tanks, 8 heavy howitzers, 12 light howitzers, 27 anti-aircraft guns between light/medium/heavy, 36 anti-tank guns, 40 mortars, 192 heavy machine guns, 378 light machine guns, 245 machine guns, 6,485 rifles. There were also: 133 motorbikes and sidecars in the Reconnaissance Battalion, 369 trucks, of which 206 Steyr 440/640s, in the Infantry Regiment, 190 trucks and tractors in the Artillery Regiment[17], 30 of which Sd.Kfz 7 8-tonne[18].

On 12 August 1944, the Armoured Regiment passed its rehearsal and completed the training run by German personnel, thus enabling the Bronirana Brigade to be declared combat-ready. In view of the completion of the training, most of the German advisers left the Brigade, replaced by a small liaison unit (DVK 162) under the command of Lieutenant Irmscher.

Even in the summer of 1944, the delivery of German arms and material to Bulgaria continued; by the end of August, several convoys with weapons, equipment, ammunition of various types and three Panzerbefehlswagen IV command tanks were on their way from Germany. Having heard of Bulgaria's probable change of alliance, the Germans, on 25 August, decided to divert the convoy loads en route to the Balkans, allocating the material to German units deployed in the Balkan area. The three Panzerbefehlswagen IV were sent to Niš where, after Bulgaria's declaration of war, they were reused by German troops.

As of 14 September 1944, the Battalions of the Armoured Regiment had all the planned tanks in service: 37 tanks and 11 trucks in the 1st and 2nd, 35 tanks and 11 trucks in the 3rd.

---

16   According to other sources, the brigade had a total strength of 9,950 men.

17   RSO/1: Yes, 40 vehicles were delivered for the motorised anti-tank battalion of the Armoured Brigade. They proved unsuitable for towing the PAK 40 guns deployed by the battalion. Eventually, the RSO/1s were used as tractors for the leFH18/leFH 18/40.motorised artillery regiment towing light 10.5 cm howitzers. The armoured brigade tested towing a 7.5 cm PaK 40 anti-tank gun, but it turned out that the tractors were slow and unsuitable for the purpose. Eventually, the Armoured Brigade found a tractor that fulfilled its requirements for towing the PAK 40. It was the Ford V3000 S/SSM 'Maultier' (Sd.Kfz. 3b) Nine vehicles were delivered to the Armoured Brigade, where they were used to tow 3.7 cm M 36 anti-aircraft guns (3.7 cm Flak 36).

18   The Sd.Kfz.7 (Sonder-Kraftfahrzeug 7 - mittlerer Zugkraftwagen 8 t) were named KM11 in the Bulgarian Army. Six Sd.Kfz. 7 were used to tow the 8.8-cm Flak cannons in the Bronirana Brigade's heavy anti-aircraft battery.

▲ Three M-222 armoured cars, just delivered by the Germans to the Bulgarian army in 1943, are still unarmed and unregistered.

▼ An M-222 armoured car, an M-223 and an M-222, belonging to the Reconnaissance Battalion of the Bronirana Brigade, in the summer of 1944.

▲ M-222 armoured car in service with the Reconnaissance Battalion of the Bronirana Brigade. In the photograph, the symbol of the Brigade, the 4 circles, and that of the Battalion, the blooming flower, are clearly visible.

▼ The first examples of Pz.Kpfw. IV Ausf. G (T-IV Maybach) delivered by the Germans to Bulgaria, one can still see the white cross painted on the side of the vehicle, which was later obliterated by the Bulgarians.

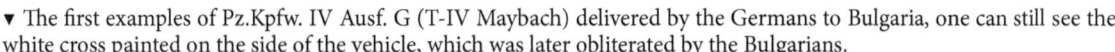

▲ Another photograph of early Pz.Kpfw. IV Ausf. G (T-IV Maybach), delivered by the Germans to Bulgaria, taken from a different side.

▼ Two T-4 Maybach tanks and an M-222 armoured car marching over muddy terrain during winter exercises in early 1944.

▲ A tank driver was photographed on board a T-4 Maybach tank, delivered a few days ago, in early 1944.

▼ One of the first Pz.Kpfw. IV Ausf. G delivered during the training of Bulgarian tank drivers.

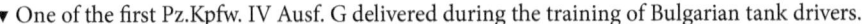

▲ A Pz.Kpfw. IV tank that had just been handed over to the 1st Armoured Regiment in the summer of 1943.

▼ A T-4 Maybach tank engaged in winter exercises in early 1944 with infantry support.

▲ T-IV Maybach tank (Pz.Kpfw. Ausf. G) during a transfer in autumn 1943.

▼ Column of StuG III filmed during a ceremony in Bulgaria at the end of 1943.

▲ StuG III just delivered by the Germans, note behind the assault guns some Renault AHN trucks.

▼ A StuG III, still with the German cross painted on the sides of the casemate, probably in service at the Niš School, surrounded by Bulgarian tank drivers in training.

▲ An 8-tonne Sd.Kfz 7 half-trailer, KM11 for the Bulgarians, in service in the Bronirana Brigada for towing 88 mm guns.

▼ T-IV Maybach tanks filmed during training in 1943.

▲ The StuG III column of the 1st SAO, shturmovo artileriĭsko otdelenie, on its way to the training camp in autumn 1943, the B60513 assault gun belonging to the Command Battery leads the column.

▼ A Hotchkiss H39 light tank, in service with the Bulgarian Gendarmerie in 1944, restored and exhibited at the National Museum of Military History in Sofia.

THE COUP D'ETAT

Having the Bronirana Brigade ready for combat, just as rumours of a possible break-up of the alliance and Bulgaria's move into the enemy camp were intensifying, suddenly became a matter of considerable concern for the OKW. A secret plan was therefore devised to put the Bulgarian armoured units out of action, using, to carry out this delicate operation, a special unit called 'Verband Collins', whose task was to sabotage all tanks and assault guns in order to prevent the Bulgarian units from fighting the German troops.

The personnel of the 'Verband Collins', consisting of instructors from the combat school in Niš, were to be concentrated at the German base in Plovdiv and then divided into four groups intended to operate against the Bulgarian units stationed at the following locations:

- Group I: in Plovdiv against the 2nd SAO with 25 StuGs. III
- 2nd and 3rd Groups: in Plovdiv and Pasardjik against the Armoured Regiment with 88 Pz.Kpfw. IV
- 4th Group: in the Sofia area against the 1st SAO equipped with 25 StuG .IIIs

The sabotage, to be carried out by the German military, consisted of removing and/or destroying critical parts that were indispensable to the operation of the vehicles. The turn of events, and the speed with which they occurred, prevented the plan from being implemented, thus leaving the Bulgarian tanks and assault guns intact and ready for use.

The government of Prime Minister Bagrjanov declared on 26 August 1944 that Bulgaria would remain neutral, despite the threat posed by the Red Army, which had almost fully occupied Romania, and began peace negotiations with the USA and the UK. The Bulgarian Communist Party, on the same day, proclaimed that the conquest of power, through a popular uprising, was its main objective. On 2 September, a new government was formed and Konstantin Muraviev was appointed Prime Minister. He continued the peace negotiations, supported new democratic reforms and ordered the withdrawal of German troops from Bulgaria. However, he also continued the fight against the partisans, did not formalise the exit from the Tripartite Pact and did not attempt to normalise relations with the Soviet Union.

The Soviet Union declared war on Bulgaria on 5 September 1944, ordering the Red Army to proceed with the invasion, which in only three days, given the total absence of resistance from Bulgarian army units, allowed the Soviets to occupy the north-western region and the main ports of Varna and Burgas. Between 5 and 8 September, the operational plan of the coup d'état was finalised, in which the partisans, combat groups of the PCB[19] and the Patriotic Front army would participate, to be carried out on the night of 9 September and which would allow Bulgaria to be taken over.

The Bronirana Brigade, whose units had been decentralised to various locations as a result of the US aerial bombardment of Sofia, was ordered to assemble all units by 5 September and take up position in the area west of the capital, with the task of guarding the road between Sofia and Niš and blocking the movement of German forces in all directions. The Brigade's movement was developed and completed by the morning of the 5th, perfectly complying with the timetable of the order received. The Exploring Battalion was instead deployed in the capital Sofia to carry out security tasks.

Pursuant to the Muraviev government's declaration to disarm the German troops stationed on Bulgarian territory, on 7 September, divisions of the Brigade clashed with retreating German motorised units near Ihtiman. The German units were disarmed and captured, the prisoners were later transferred to Sofia.

---

19   Bulgarian Communist Party.

An essential contribution to the success of the coup was made by the units belonging to the Bronirana Brigada, where some officers serving in the Armoured Regiment had been in contact for some time with members of the 'Zveno' movement[20], the main actor in the uprising. The officers most involved were Major Bosilkov, Battalion Commander, and Captains Tsenov, Petrov and Slavkov, all Company Commanders. In the early afternoon of 8 September, an officer belonging to "Zveno", who was liaising with the insurgent leadership (Georgiev and Velchev), came to Captain Tsenov to inform him that the armoured regiment, in full combat gear, was to be ready to move out by the hour, informing him that he would be back by the evening to notify the commanding officer of the coup d'état. At 6 p.m. the officer returned and notified Tsenov of the password.

From 4.30 p.m., the Bronirana Brigade was on high alert on the orders of Colonel Genov, under the command of the Minister of War General Marinov. At 11.30 p.m. the armoured column led by the Company under the command of Captain Tesnov moved in the direction of Sofia. At 2.30 a.m. on 9 September, the column reached Orlov Most, the Bridge of Eagles, in the centre of the capital, where it stopped to await further orders.

After a few minutes of waiting, officers from the General Staff and the Reserve arrived and assigned the tankers of the Armoured Regiment to control and defend the Ministry of War, the Ministry of Finance, the Ministry of the Interior, the Stock Exchange, the National Assembly, the Government Palace, the Central Station, the Radio Sofia headquarters and other government office buildings. Tanks were also deployed in the Borisova Garden, at the State Mint and at strategic intersections and areas of the capital.

During the night, Captain Tsenov was the officer who continuously maintained contact between the insurgent command and the Bronirana Brigade.

On the morning of 9 September, the new government was formed, which appointed Kimon Georgiev, leader of the 'Zveno' party, as Prime Minister. On the same day, he immediately demanded an armistice from the Soviet Union and declared war on Nazi Germany.

In the days immediately following the coup, the Bronirana Brigada was deployed to protect the capital Sofia to deal with a hypothetical German attack from the Yugoslav Pirot - Niš area. The Armoured Regiment, deployed with its tanks in the capital with the task of preventing possible counter-attacks by Nazi loyalists, also rejoined the Brigada in the first days after the coup.

THE FIRST PHASE OF THE PATRIOTIC WAR

After declaring war on Germany, the Government placed the forces of the Bulgarian Army at the disposal of the 3rd Ukrainian Front, commanded by Marshal Fyodor Ivanovič Tolbuchin. The purging of the royalist component within the Armed Forces also began, including the replacement of most of the officers with soldiers linked or sympathetic to the communist regime. The change of most middle and senior officers initially created situations of indiscipline in many departments, so it was necessary to resort to returning many of the previously purged officers to service.

The commander of the Bronirana Brigada, Colonel Genov, was dismissed on 13 September, and in his place was the reserve colonel Stoyan Konstantinov Trendafilov, promoted to major-general. The commander of the Armoured Regiment, Lieutenant Colonel Dikov, was promoted to colonel.

The Bronirana Brigada, one of the few fully equipped and trained units in the Bulgarian army, had in mid-September: 88 Maybach T-IV tanks, 36 Škoda 35s and T-11s, 10 Praga, 20 M-222 and M-223 armoured cars.

---

20   The 'Zveno' movement was a Bulgarian organisation with political and military aims, founded in 1930 by army officers and intellectuals. Colonels Damjan Velčev and Kimon Georgiev, leaders of Zveno, were the architects of the coup d'état that imposed a dictatorship in Bulgaria in 1934. In 1944, Zveno joined the Patriotic Front and collaborated in the coup that overthrew the monarchy.

▲ Two Maybach T-IV tanks deployed in a square in the capital on 9 September 1944 during the coup d'état.

▼ Colonel General Damyan Velchev, Minister of Defence from September 1944 after the coup d'état, visiting an army department in autumn 1944.

▲ An American B-24 'Liberator' bomber filmed during one of the bombing raids on Bulgaria's capital, Sofia, in early 1944.

The Armoured Regiment, under the command of Colonel Dikov, was assigned in support of the 1st Bulgarian Army, with the task of advancing in the direction of Pirot - Niš and repelling the Germans. Colliding with the German rearguard during a reconnaissance in the Pirot area, a Škoda Š-35 was pinned down by anti-tank gun fire, while a Maybach T-IV was also put out of action, although the tank was later recovered and repaired at the field workshop.

During the fighting in support of the Bulgarian 35th Infantry Regiment, on 17 September, due to poor reconnaissance activity, the companies of the 2nd Battalion, commanded by Lieutenant Colonel Alexander Bosilkov, and the 3rd Battalion, commanded by Captain Ivan Gyumbabov, ended up in a minefield in the Milin Kamŭk area. Because of the mines, anti-tank gun fire and artillery, it was the 7th Company, equipped with Maybach T-IVs, that was particularly hard hit, as it lost, between destroyed and damaged tanks, 10 tanks.

In just two days, the Brigade lost 41 tank men, dead and wounded, and 11 tanks!

On 23 September, the Bronirana Brigada was assigned to the 2nd Bulgarian Army and was ordered to move in the direction of the Bulgarian-Serbian border, a movement it completed by the evening of 28 September. The offensive, drawn up by the Soviet, Bulgarian and Yugoslav Commands, called for units belonging to the 1st, 2nd and 4th Bulgarian Army to develop attacks against the German units deployed in defence of the Leskovac-Niš area and in eastern Macedonia.

The attack of the Bulgarian armed forces began on 28 September, when units of the 2nd Army, commanded by General K. Stanchev, advanced from the assembly area southwest of Pirot towards the Leskovac-Niš area, where the Germans had moved the 7. SS-Freiwilligen-Gebirgs-Division "Prinz Eugen", with the task of taking over the defence of the town of Niš and the area from Zajecar in the north to Leskovac in the south.

The first offensive action was repelled by the Germans without much difficulty, but, on 30 September,

Bulgarian scout units, together with Yugoslav partisan formations, succeeded in conquering Vlasotince, overpowering the defence made up of units of Cetnics and Serbian border guards. On 6 October, the town was recaptured by the 'Prinz Eugen' units, which had taken control of the defensive line with the arrival of all its units.

Recognising the difficulties in continuing the advance towards Niš, which was currently blocked, the Command of the 2nd Bulgarian Army ordered the Bronirana Brigada to transfer its units to the north and to attack and take Vlasotince and Bela Palanka. On 8 October, the Bronirana Brigada went into action for the first time since its establishment, carrying out a scouting attack with an armoured unit, supported by artillery, against the German defensive positions deployed south-east of Bela Palanka. The attack was repulsed in the afternoon by the 2nd Battalion of the 13th Waffen-Gebirgs-Division der SS "Handschar", which forced the Bulgarian tanks to retreat.

The 9th and part of the 10th of October were used by the Bulgarian commandos to reinforce the units for the new attack. On the day of the 10th, after substantial and careful preparation by the artillery and the support of Soviet fighter-bombers, the Brigada attack, led by 60 tanks followed by infantry, began, hitting the German defensive line. The attack was successful, the German defensive lines were overrun and the banks of the Morava River were reached.

The town of Vlasotince was recaptured, after fierce fighting, by a 21-tank armoured unit and motorised infantry, belonging to the Bronirana Brigada. Despite the presence of numerous 5 cm PaK 38 anti-tank guns, deployed by the Germans in strategic positions to defend the city, the Bulgarian tanks managed to overcome the anti-tank defences and defeat the enemy. The German soldiers, belonging to the 3rd Battalion of the 13th Waffen-Gebirgs-Division der SS "Handschar", were forced to retreat, falling back to Ravna Dubrava, after suffering heavy losses.

The entire front line in the meantime was moving, with the German units beginning to retreat in the direction of Niš and towards the bridges over the Morava to the western bank of the river. On the morning of 12 October, in order to test the resistance of the new German defensive positions, a combat group of the Bronirana Brigada, consisting of 12 Maybach T-IV tanks, carried out an attack in the area of Bela Palanka, but lost five tanks, two of which were destroyed by the 8.8-cm FlaK guns. While the fighting was taking place in Bela Palanka, the bulk of the Bronirana Brigada was busy, further to the south-west, supporting the attack led by the 15th Brigade of the 47th Partisan Division, which, in the late morning, managed to liberate Leskovac. The success allowed the Brigade's reconnaissance battalion to cross the Morava River, a movement that was followed by the rest of the units in the late evening.

On 13 October, the Bronirana Brigada formed two combat groups: the Dikov group, named after its commander, consisting of the 1st armoured company, an artillery unit, a motorised company and a StuG III company, and the Mutafov group, commander of the unit, with the 2nd armoured company. Crossing the Morava allowed the Bronirana Brigada to travel along the western bank of the river, which allowed it, after crossing Brestovac, to position its units, on the morning of the 14th, on the heights surrounding the village of Merosina, where the HQ of the 7. SS-Freiwilligen-Gebirgs-Division "Prinz Eugen" following the retreat from Niš carried out the same day. Taking advantage of the favourable position and surprise, the tanks and artillery of the Brigade immediately opened fire, destroying all the vehicles belonging to the 'Prinz Eugen' HQ, as well as the houses in the village where the personnel were quartered.

Thinking that they could easily conquer the newly bombed village, the Bronirana Brigade Command ordered the infantry to assault, an attack that was repulsed with heavy losses. During the day, the

'Prinz Eugen' units, which had previously been scattered over a wide area, regrouped in Merosina to organise a counter-attack, which was suspended as the German Division was ordered to retreat in a north-westerly direction.

With the retreat of the 'Prinz Eugen', the Bronirana Brigade had the way clear, as did the other units belonging to the 2nd Bulgarian Army, to proceed to the liberation of Kosovo, an objective set for the Bulgarian Army by the 3rd Ukrainian Front Command.

The Headquarters of Army Group E (Heeresgruppe E) of the German Army, which was engaged in the retreat of the units from Greece, was fully aware that if the enemy troops broke through the defensive lines and conquered Kosovo, the main northward route of march: Skopje - Pristina - Mitrovica - Kraljevo would be blocked, with the consequence that all German units coming from the south would be stopped and forced to surrender.

The German Command reacted quickly to this serious threat, quickly setting up a combat group, under the command of Colonel Langer, consisting of several infantry companies, a company of cyclists, an anti-tank company and a battery of hippotrained artillery[21]. Kampfgruppe Langer was given the task of blocking and holding the Prepolac Pass, located approximately 36 kilometres north of Pristina, for as long as possible.

While German preparations to block the Prepolac pass were in full swing, the Bronirana Brigade was ordered to move south-west along the Prokuplje - Kursumlija road. Between 15 and 18 October, heavy fighting took place for the liberation of the town of Prokuplje, which was liberated on 16 October, and the town of Kuršumlija, which was evacuated by the Germans after heavy night fighting on 17 October.

In the town of Kursumlija, the Bronirana Brigada established its headquarters and began the scouting and reconnaissance activities of its units. The motorbike companies, belonging to the Reconnaissance Battalion, were sent southwards in the direction of Rača, while the 12-vehicle armoured car company, under the command of Major Dimitrov, was also sent southwards, but on a parallel road, in the direction of Kuršumlijska Banja, a town located 18 km from Podujevo.

It was precisely at Kuršumlijska Banja that the first clashes took place between the scouting units of the Bronirana Brigada and the Germans of Kampfgruppe Langer. The fighting was immediately very hard and violent, an infantry regiment of the 4th Bulgarian Division intervened in support of the Brigada, which, however, had to suffer heavy losses without being able to break through the German defensive line. On 21 October, the 9th company, operating in support of the infantry units of the 4th Division, carried out an attack on the heights around the village of Merdare, which was repelled by German fire that also destroyed the tank of Lieutenant Viniciy Petrov, the company commander.

The Command of the 2nd Army, seeing the deadlocked situation, ordered the 6th Infantry Division to reach the front and take part in the attack against the German forces defending the Prepolac Pass. The transfer of the Division was carried out by truck, but the area was already clogged with the vehicles of the other divisions and further congested the transfer operations and preparation for the attack.

Despite the arrival of reinforcements, the advance of the Bronirana Brigada, which was used as an armoured battering ram to conquer the pass, could not be realised, mainly due to the orography of the terrain, which was mountainous with roads with steep embankments on both sides.

Thanks to the favourable orography and the combativeness of the Kampfgruppe units, Colonel

---

21 Many units of Kampfgruppe Langer belonged to the II./IR16 - 22. Infanterie-Division previously stationed in Crete.

Langer was able to hold the Prepolac pass for three weeks, blocking the Bulgarian advance towards Kosovo and allowing the retreating German formations from Greece to complete their retreat, even with their heavy armament and equipment in tow.

The Bronirana Brigada resumed its attacks against the Germans at the Prepolac Pass on 1 November, although it did not develop its greatest efforts until the 3rd. On 4 November, units of the 4th Bulgarian Infantry Division finally managed to break through the German positions defending the adjacent Merdare pass. On 5 November, after managing with great difficulty to advance a few armoured units on the heights surrounding the Prepolac Pass, the Bronirana Brigade overcame the defensive lines held by German soldiers belonging to the 734th Jäger-Regiment of the 104. Jäger-Division, conquering the Prepolac Pass and heading towards Podujevo with a mass of 60 tanks.

The town of Podujevo was liberated from the Germans on 5 November by the Bronirana Brigada, which, however, lost numerous tanks in the attack, mainly due to the 8.8 cm FlaK cannons manoeuvred by Luftwaffe soldiers engaged in the defence of the town. At least six tanks were put out of action near the railway station. The terrain on which the fighting took place, which was mainly mountainous and impassable, put the Brigade's tanks to the test. The performance of the Czechoslovak Škoda Š-35, T-11 and 'Praga' tanks was highly appreciated by the tank crews, and by the infantry. They brilliantly overcame the roughness and reached positions considered unreachable by the German defenders, enabling the Bulgarian troops to overcome the defences and win the battles.

Having liberated Podujevo, the Bronirana Brigade continued its advance south-west along the road to Pristina, in pursuit of the retreating German units. However, the German rearguard put up fierce resistance, which was not properly considered by the brigade's command, and the brigade was thus forced to retreat back to Podujevo, where it remained available while awaiting orders from the 2nd Army. Two columns were formed, with the armoured divisions as spearheads, to carry out simultaneous attacks in the direction of Pristina and Mitrovica, but despite the soldiers' efforts, no results were achieved in the following two weeks. In the fierce fighting that developed during the attacks against the German defensive positions, the armoured units engaged in the conquest of Pristina lost 12 tanks in close combat with grenadiers belonging to the IR16 of the 22. Infanterie-Division north-west of the city.

On 19 November, the Bronirana Brigada was fully assembled near Bellopojë, 16 km north of Pristina. On 20 November, the vanguards of the Brigada clashed with the German rearguard defending Donje Ljupče, which was equipped with numerous anti-tank guns and sheltered by minefields.

The commander of the 3rd Battalion, Lieutenant Colonel Momchilov, decided to outflank the defence by crossing the Kopaonik mountains, although the very steep slopes and poor visibility due to the autumn fog were undoubtedly not favourable conditions for the tanks. Spurred on by their commander, the tank drivers set their vehicles in motion and climbed the steep slopes, and, despite the strain on their engines, managed to reach the top of the hill and plunge in behind the defenders, thus overrunning the German defensive line and breaking the front, at the cost of four tanks destroyed or damaged. Again, the successful outcome of the battle was due to the Škoda tanks. Having crossed the German defensive line, the Bronirana Brigada participated in the attack that liberated the city of Pristina on the 21st.

After helping to liberate Pristina, the Brigade reached Vučitrn, 23 km northwest of Pristina, where it reorganised in preparation for the attack on Kosovska Mitrovica.

The attack that led to the liberation of Kosovska Mitrovica was successfully carried out on 22

November. After taking part in the liberation of Kosovska Mitrovica, the Bronirana Brigade was withdrawn from the front and reached Podujevo, where it remained at the disposal of the Bulgarian 2nd Army, maintaining and repairing its vehicles, worn out after months of moving and fighting, and making up for losses in men and material. Although sources vary in their numbers, it is possible that in Mitrovica alone, the Brigade lost about 20 tanks, which were effectively beyond repair, because there were no spare parts left.

With the liberation of Mitrovica, the operational cycle of the units belonging to the 2nd Bulgarian Army in Yugoslavia came to an end. Between the end of November and the beginning of December 1944, all Bulgarian units were assembled in Serbia and prepared to return to Bulgaria

The Bronirana Brigade, having assembled all its units, also returned home at the end of November, parading in full in Sofia on 2 December 1944 amidst two wings of a jubilant population.

Also participating in the fighting against the Germans in Yugoslavia were the two SAOs, shturmovo artileriĭsko otdelenie, the 1st in support of the units belonging to the 2nd Bulgarian Army, the 2nd to the units belonging to the 1st Bulgarian Army.

The 1st SAO was used in support of the infantry in the fighting for the conquest of Bela Palanka, Niš, Poduevo, Mitrovica, Vuchi Trun, during which some vehicles were hit by Soviet assault aircraft by mistake. The 2nd SAO was mainly engaged in the fighting in the direction of Kumanovo and Kriva Palanka, while, in support of a company of paratroopers, it took part in the battles for Strazhin. On 28 October, he provided supporting fire to the 6th Infantry Regiment engaged against the 11th. Luftwaffen-Feld-Division. Once through the German defensive lines, the two SAOs continued to support the infantry in the pursuit of the retreating Germans.

During the Yugoslav campaign, the two SAOs lost a total of 4 StuG IIIs in the fighting, 3 belonging to the 2nd SAO and 1 to the 1st SAO. Between the end of November and the beginning of December, the two SAOs returned to Bulgaria, some StuG IIIs took part in the parade on 2 December in the capital Sofia.

In total, the Bronirana Brigade, from 28 September to 23 October 1944, had 47 tanks out of action, of which at least 30 were due to breakdowns during transfers, with most of those destroyed or damaged in combat lost from the Niš area to Kursumlija. Another dozen tanks were lost in the attack on Podujevo, another 12 in the liberation of Pristina. According to other sources, 20 tanks were believed to have been totally destroyed during the first phase of the Patriotic War.

Thus, in early December 1944, the operational activity of the Bronirana Brigade came to an end. Despite the problems caused by the poor quality of its training, which had been highlighted during manoeuvres in 1943 and early 1944, and the mediocre value of its tanks, it carried out a fair amount of action in Yugoslavia between October and November 1944, achieving good results in the field, facing experienced and combative German units.

The Bronirana Brigada never faced German armoured units during the Yugoslavian campaign, which probably allowed it to avoid heavy losses when facing better tanks and experienced crews, but it was equally feared by the German infantry for its combativeness and ability to use its technologically outdated tanks in the valleys and mountains of Serbia and Kosovo in the autumn of 1944, in areas where it was difficult to move and manoeuvre with such means.

▲ The Škoda B60033 tank and the Praga B60062, B60066, B60065 and B60068 tanks waiting to take part in the parade on 2 December 1944 in Sofia. Note the colouring of the various St Andrew's Crosses painted on the turrets of the vehicles.

▲ A Škoda LT vz. 35, a veteran of the fighting in Yugoslavia during the first phase of the Patriotic War, parades in Sofia during the December 1944 parade. Note the inscription 'Mitrovica' on the front of the vehicle in memory of the fighting for the liberation of the town.

▼ Škoda LT vz. 35, 'Praga' and T-4 Maybach ready to parade in Sofia on 2 December 1944. In the foreground one can see the rectangle painted in white, right on the Škoda's turret, as an aerial identification sign, it is one of the few photographs in which such a sign is identified on a Bulgarian tank.

▲ Škoda T-11 and LT vz. 35 belonging to the 7th Company, returning to Sofia in December 1944.

▼ MW R75 motorcars and M-222 armoured car of the Reconnaissance Battalion during operations in Kosovo against the Germans in October 1944.

▲ Tank 'Praga' B60065, belonging to 9th Company, parades in Sofia during the parade on 2 December 1944.

▲ Photograph of the rear of tank 'Praga' B60062, belonging to 9th Company, during the parade in Sofia on 2 December 1944. One can clearly see the positions of the St Andrew's Crosses painted in black around the turret, the plate and the holes on the exhaust pipe caused by the fighting in Yugoslavia.

▼ Tank 'Praga' B60062, belonging to the 9th Company, parades in Sofia on 2 December 1944 on its return from fighting in Yugoslavia during the first phase of the Patriotic War.

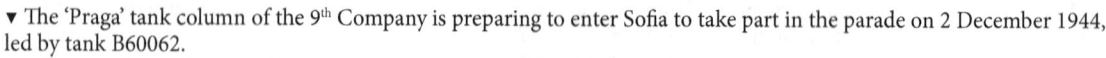

▲ Škoda tank, equipped with A-3 cannon, belonging to the 8th Company during the parade on 2 December 1944 in Sofia.

▼ The 'Praga' tank column of the 9th Company is preparing to enter Sofia to take part in the parade on 2 December 1944, led by tank B60062.

▲ Another photograph of tank 'Praga' B60062 taken during the parade in Sofia on 2 December 1944.

▼ T-IV Maybach tank (Pz.Kpfw. Ausf. G) belonging to the 1st Armoured Regiment during training in the winter of 1943/1944.

▲ A T-4 Maybach belonging to the Bronirana Brigada advancing inside Macedonia in autumn 1944.

▼ T-IV Maybach tank during the parade in Sofia on 2 December 1944.

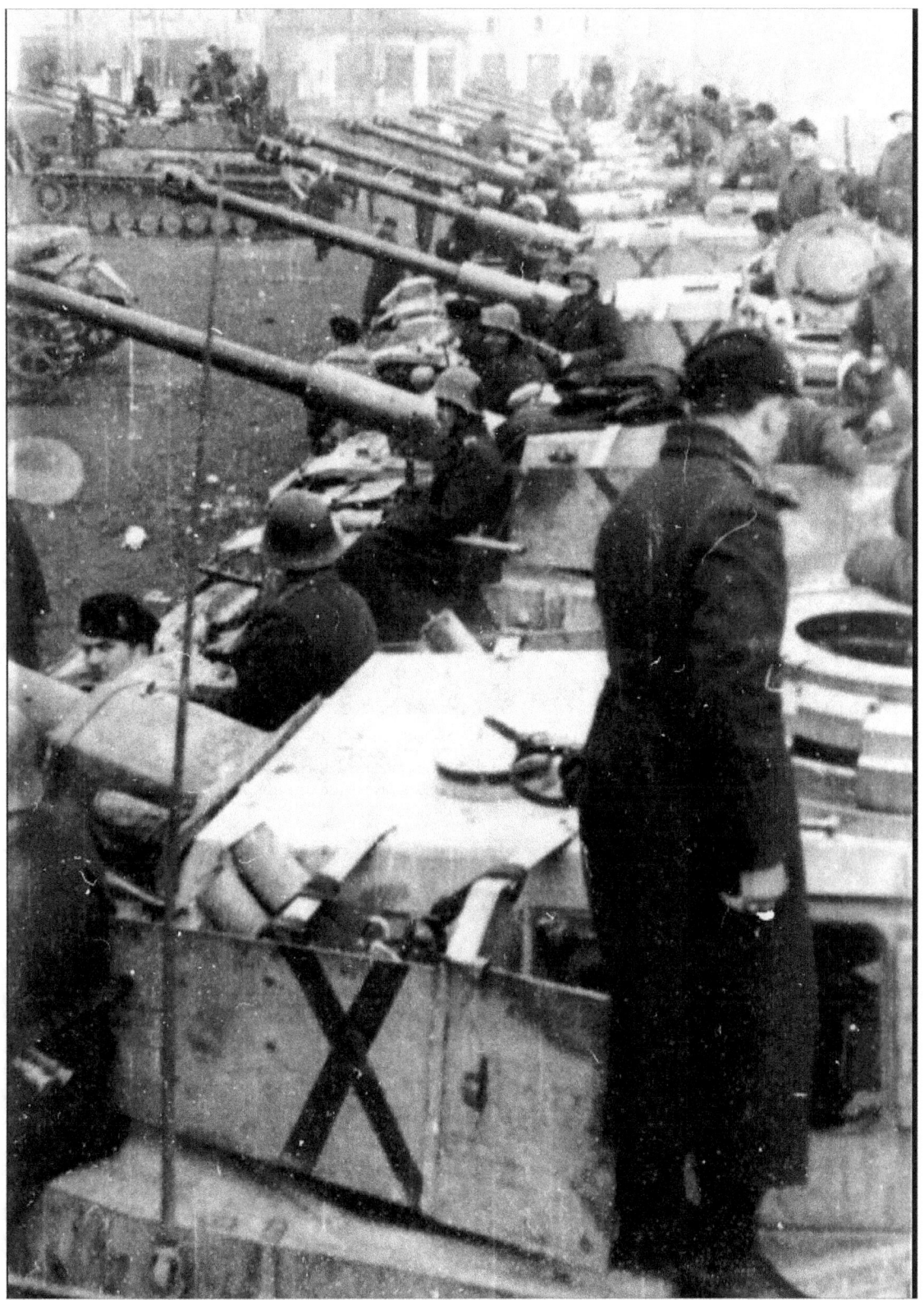

▲ T-IV Maybach tank (Pz.Kpfw. Ausf. H), distinguished by a black number 13 bordered in white on the front of the casemate, parades in Sofia on 2 December 1944.

▲ One of the few T-4 Maybach tanks covered in zimmerit in service in the Bronirana Brigada.

▼ Column of T-IV Maybach tanks in the square around the cathedral 'St. Aleksandr Nevsky' prepare to parade on 2 December 1944 in the capital Sofia, in the foreground the B60280 tank. Note the position of the St. Andrew's Cross on the schurzen and hull, and the infantrymen carried on the tanks like the Soviets.

▲ Military Academy cadets pose on a Maybach T-4 in Sofia in autumn 1944.

▼ Column of StuG IIIs marching to the front in the autumn of 1944 in Yugoslavia during the first phase of the Patriotic War, led by vehicle B60522, belonging to the 2nd SAO.

▲ The StuG III Ausf. G B60506, belonging to 1st Battery of the 1st SAO, at a halt during the war in Yugoslavia in autumn 1944.

▲ The StuG III Ausf. G B60512, belonging to the 1st Battery of the 1st SAO, during the parade in Sofia on 2 December 1944.

▼ The StuG III Ausf. G B60539, belonging to the 2nd SAO, parked after the Battle of Kryva Palanka in October 1944 in Yugoslavia.

▲ A StuG III walks through the streets of Sofia before taking part in the parade on 2 December 1944, note the Bulgarian flag spread over the casemate.

▼ Back of a StuG III assault gun engaged in Yugoslavia during the first phase of the Patriotic War. One can clearly see the position of the St. Andrew's Cross painted in black directly on the hull and the registration number painted in white by hand. Unfortunately, it is not possible to read the number plate completely: B6053?, which in any case corresponds to a vehicle belonging to the 2nd SAO.

▲ Back of a StuG III assault gun engaged in Yugoslavia during the first phase of the Patriotic War. One can clearly see the position of the St. Andrew's Cross painted in black on a white square.

▼ A StuG III assault cannon supports infantry during the fighting for the liberation of Macedonia, during the first phase of the Patriotic War, near Strazhin in October 1944.

▲ Colonel Martin Dikov, commander of the Bronirana Brigade Armoured Regiment since September 1944.

▲ A StuG III during refuelling, shell and fuel operations during the fighting in Yugoslavia in autumn 1944. The black St. Andrew's Cross edged in white painted on the back of the hull can be seen.

▼ Column of M-223 armoured cars, in the foreground, and M-222 belonging to the Reconnaissance Battalion of the Bronirana Brigade waiting to return to Sofia in December 1944.

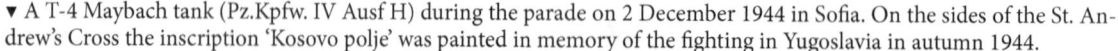

▲ The Steyr 1500A, B10351, belonging to the Bronirana Brigade HQ, during the parade on 2 December in Sofia, the officer in the foreground is Major General Stoyan Konstantinov Trendafilov, commander of the Brigade.

▼ A T-4 Maybach tank (Pz.Kpfw. IV Ausf H) during the parade on 2 December 1944 in Sofia. On the sides of the St. Andrew's Cross the inscription 'Kosovo polje' was painted in memory of the fighting in Yugoslavia in autumn 1944.

▲ A StuG III, with a group of infantrymen on board, engaged in fighting in Yugoslavia in autumn 1944.

▼ A German magnetic mine, thrown at a StuG III belonging to the 2nd SAO during the fighting in Yugoslavia in October 1944, did not explode, a sapper is removing it.

▲ Bulgarian troops, supported by a StuG III, entered Kriva Palanka, Macedonia, in October 1944 after breaking through the defence of German troops.

THE SECOND PHASE OF THE PATRIOTIC WAR

When the campaign ended with the liberation of Kosovo, the units of the 1st, 2nd and 4th Bulgarian Army returned to Bulgaria, partly as a result of strong pressure from the Yugoslav side, which did not want the Bulgarians, who had occupied parts of Yugoslavia for three years following the 1941 conflict, to remain on their territory.

The Bronirana Brigade was also withdrawn from the front and returned home, to be reorganised and re-equipped following the heavy losses suffered in men and vehicles. It should be emphasised that, especially with regard to vehicles, the lack of spare parts for Czechoslovak and German tanks was impossible to fill, except with the contribution of the Soviet Union, where there were hundreds of tanks, such as those in service with the Brigade, captured from the Germans and in good condition. In December 1944, the Bulgarian government took the decision to continue fighting against the Nazis alongside the Red Army and, thanks to the support obtained from Stalin, Tito could not oppose it. Thus, the Bulgarian 1st Army was formed within the 3rd Ukrainian Front under the command of General Fyodor Ivanovič Tolbuchin. The Bulgarian 1st Army was assembled in January 1945 in south-western Hungary, ready to be deployed along the Drava River.

As the Bronirana Brigade was being reorganised, an independent Armoured Battalion was nevertheless established, with personnel and vehicles from the Brigade, to be included among the units serving in the 1st Army.

The 1st Armoured Battalion, under the command of Major Ivan Gyumbabov, consisted of:
- Headquarters: 2 Maybach T-IV tanks
- 1st Company: 10 Maybach T-IV tanks

- 2nd Company: 10 Maybach T-IV tanks
- Reconnaissance Company: 2 M-222 and 1 M-223 armoured car
- Services: motorbikes, cars and trucks

The 1st Armoured Battalion was ordered to move to the area around the Hungarian city of Pécs in January 1945, to supplement the defensive positions already present in the area. The transfer to Pécs was very difficult, due to numerous vehicle breakdowns on the way, which affected most of the tanks, which had to undergo numerous repairs lasting several days.

According to the organisational directives issued by the Soviet Command regarding the formation of an armoured battalion, it was to consist of one heavy and two medium tank companies, as well as having an assault gun company.

Faced with the Soviet Command's request for the completion of the Armoured Battalion's staff, the Bulgarian Army Command replied that it was unable to set up the Heavy Tank Company as it did not have such means at its disposal, thus requesting the Soviets to hand over suitable German tanks, which they had captured and stored in the Red Army's depots.

A clarification must be made concerning the delivery of materials by the Red Army to the Bulgarian army and, in particular, the armoured vehicles supplied to the Bronirana Brigada. In the Soviet depots there were hundreds of German, Hungarian, Romanian and Italian tanks and assault guns, captured intact or damaged on the battlefields, especially following the victorious offensives from 1943 onwards. All captured combat-capable vehicles were overhauled, painted in classic Soviet green and returned to service, even in organic Red Army units.

The main Soviet tank, the T-34, was delivered to the Bulgarian units only in the last month of the war: two T-34/85s for training. The vehicles handed over by the Red Army to the Bronirana Brigade and the Armoured Battalion serving in the Bulgarian 1st Army were tanks and assault guns, or self-propelled guns, captured from the enemy and present in the depots of the 3rd Ukrainian Front, which was entrusted with the delivery.

As of 1 January 1945, the Army General Staff decreed the independence of the armoured troops, separating them from the mechanised troops. It was the official birth of the Bulgarian tank troops! In January 1945, while the Bronirana Brigada was reorganising its units, with which the independent Armoured Battalion had also been formed, the 2nd Armoured Brigade was established with headquarters in Plovdiv, although at the time without any means. The Brigade's tank situation was also extremely critical, as most of the vehicles in charge were obsolete and no longer suitable for combat, but only usable for training.

The month of March 1945 was particularly intense for the Bulgarian armoured units.

In Bulgaria, the Bronirana Brigada proceeded to overhaul the tanks in service, declaring that the following vehicles: 32 Maybach T-IV, 13 Škoda Š-35 and 3 'Praga' were no longer repairable and were decommissioned and disposed of. The 13 Škodas, after recovering their armament, were sent to the foundry to recover precious metal.

In mid-March, the 1st SAO and 2nd SAO, with their men and the few remaining StuG IIIs ready for combat, were included in the 2nd Armoured Brigade in formation in Plovdiv.

On 6 March, the 6th SS Armoured Army, the 2nd Armoured Army and Heeresgruppe E, began the offensives planned in Operation 'Frühlingserwachen', the last major German attack on the Eastern Front in an attempt to recapture the Hungarian oil area south-east of Lake Balaton. Against the Bulgarian troops deployed in defence of the north bank of the Drava River, units belonging to the 2nda Armoured Army and Heeresgruppe E.

Near Donji Miholjac, the 3rd Bulgarian Infantry Division was forced to retreat after its defensive lines were overrun by German tanks. On 7 March, a counterattack was carried out by the Bulgarian units, reinforced by the Armoured Battalion, which had 25 Maybach T-IVs, and units belonging to the reserve of the 1st Army.

The Armoured Battalion clashed against German units belonging to the 104. Jäger-Division and the 297. Infanterie-Division. The Bulgarian tank advance made some initial progress, but in close combat with the German infantry, five tanks were destroyed and the counterattack was first blocked and then repulsed. It then took part in the defensive battles near Dravasobolch and Dravapolkonya, playing its role in supporting the Bulgarian infantry until 16 March, when the Red Army's counter-offensive began, pushing the Germans back towards Austria.

The Armoured Battalion, following heavy losses, including destroyed or damaged tanks, was then sent to the rear for necessary reorganisation.

The 3rd Ukrainian Front Command decided in mid-March 1945 to supply some armoured vehicles to restore the losses suffered by the Independent Armoured Battalion. The following were delivered: 1 Pz.Kpfw. IV, 2 StuG III Ausf. G, 1 Stug Ausf. F, 1 StuH 42 assault howitzer, 1 Jagdpanzer IV/70(V), 1 Jagdpanzer IV, 4 Jagdpanzer 38(t) Hetzer[22], 2 Italian L40 self-propelled tanks[23], 1 Hungarian Turan I tank[24]. With the received assault guns and self-propelled vehicles, a battery was formed and included in the staff of one of the two companies of the Armoured Battalion. At the beginning of April, with the arrival of new crews from Bulgaria, the battery was taken out of the Armoured Battalion and formed an independent artillery assault unit.

On 17 March 1945, the Soviet Command finally decided to hand over the means to establish the Heavy Armoured Company, the third company of the Independent Armoured Battalion. A Pz.Kpfw.V "Panther" tank[25] was handed over to the Bulgarian tankers, with which to begin training. At the end of March, the tank drivers, who were to train the crews of the Panther T-V Heavy Armoured Company stationed in Hungary, were selected from those belonging to the 1st Armoured Brigade in formation in Sofia, from where they left to join the Battalion in Hungary.

Arriving at the front on 11 April, the tank drivers took delivery of 14 Panther T-V tanks from the Soviet military on the 13th at the Pana Deveger -Szombathely area. The new Heavy Armoured Company was assigned to the command of Lieutenant Georgi Botev Ivanov[26]. Training of the tank drivers and the Company began immediately with the help of Soviet instructors. Training on the new tank proceeded intensively, although the Bulgarian tank drivers encountered problems with the Soviet radio equipment, which had replaced the original German ones.

The Bulgarian Commands made several requests to the 3rd Ukrainian Front Command to obtain the original German radio equipment removed by the Soviets from the Panther Vs, to replace those now in service. However, there is no certainty that the original radio equipment was delivered by the Soviets to the Bulgarian tankers.

The complexity of the training, and the short time available, meant that the end of the war came before the Bulgarian crews finished training, so the Heavy Armoured Company was unable to enter service and participate in the final fighting of the Second World War.

---

22   The Jagdpanzer 38(t) Hetzer fighters in Bulgaria were named 'Praga' assault guns.
23   The Italian L40 self-propelled vehicles equipped with a 47/32 cannon in Bulgaria were named SPA self-propelled cannon.
24   The Hungarian Turan I tank in Bulgaria was named the Wenger tank.
25   The Pz.Kpfw.V 'Panther' tank in Bulgaria was named 'boyna kola Panther T-V', commonly abbreviated to 'Panther' T-V.
26   According to other sources, the commander was Lieutenant Georgi Botev Shinkov.

At the end of May 1945, the Heavy Armoured Company, with all 15 Panther T-V tanks, was loaded onto a railway convoy for transfer to Sofia, where it became part of the 2nd Armoured Brigade stationed in Plovdiv.

In April, the overhaul of the tanks in service continued in Bulgaria, more tanks were decommissioned: 21 R35 tanks, 3 'Vickers' tanks and 9 CV33 fast tanks, while 7 'Praga' were modified into armoured ambulances and supply vehicles. The last 5 CV33 and 19 R35 were transferred to the Training Companies.

The 1st Independent Armoured Battalion, after reorganising its units and restoring the efficiency of its vehicles, took part in the breakthrough of the German defence line Margit in the first ten days of April, losing 11 tanks in the hard fighting, including destroyed and damaged tanks. On 15 April, it participated, together with the 47th Infantry Regiment and a platoon of paratroopers, in the fighting for the capture of the village of Yastrebtsi. The village was captured, but five more tanks were damaged.

During the night, the Germans launched three counter-attacks to retake the village, but were always repulsed. The battalion's armoured units stopped along the road to Zashevac at around noon on 16 April to rest, but were suddenly hit by numerous mortar shells that caused numerous deaths and injuries. Among the dead were also the Battalion commander, Major Ivan Gumbabov, and the commander of the parachute company, Major Lyubomir Noev.

Captain Vasil Taralezhkov, former commander of the 1st SAO, assumed command of the battalion. The 1st Independent Armoured Battalion, having completed this last operational cycle, was withdrawn from the front and placed among the reserve units of the Bulgarian III Army Corps, where it used all available means to repair damaged tanks. He remained at the disposal of the 1st Bulgarian Army Command until the end of the conflict, but did not participate in any further combat.

As of 1 May, 11 tanks and 6 assault guns were in service.

From the second half of April 1945, several units belonging to the Bronirana Brigada were also deployed north of Varaždin, at the disposal of the 3rd Army Corps, belonging to the Bulgarian 1st Army, which was fighting for the liberation of Hungary from the Nazis. During the final offensive against the German troops, they clashed against units of the 13th Waffen-Gebirgs-Division der SS "Handschar" north of Varaždin.

On 13 May 1945, the Bronirana Brigade ended its war operations in the town of Nagykanizsa, where it encountered British troops that had entered Austria from the south on the Italian border.

In the second fortnight of May, the units belonging to the Bulgarian 1st Army concentrated near the town of Katoshwar, from where they began their return to Bulgaria.

A number of damaged Bulgarian tanks were sent to Austrian specialised workshops in Vienna for repairs and were returned to Bulgaria in August 1945.

▲ T-IV Maybach tank, belonging to the Armoured Battalion, during the advance into Hungary in the second phase of the Patriotic War, on the schurzen one can see the coat of arms with the Bulgarian flag painted diagonally.

▼ T-IV Maybach tank (Pz.Kpfw. Ausf. H or J) belonging to the Armoured Battalion during the second phase of the Patriotic War, in May 1945 in Pecs, Hungary. Note the large red stars edged in white painted on the front hull and on the schurzen on either side of the turret as a sign of recognition.

▲ Another photograph taken from above of the 'Panther' barracks in Sofia in May 1945, one can clearly see on the first tank, covered in zimmerit, the red star edged in white and the Company's coat of arms, a white dog.

▼ A Jagdpanzer 38(t) 'Hetzer' tank fighter, serving in the Bulgarian Armoured Battalion during the second phase of the Patriotic War, in May 1945 in Pecs, Hungary. Note the large red stars edged in white painted on the sides of the casemate as a sign of recognition.

▲ A Jagdpanzer IV fighter and a Turan II tank in service with the Bulgarian Armoured Battalion in the spring of 1945. These were vehicles captured by the Soviets and given to Bulgaria to replace vehicles lost in combat.

▼ A Renault UE chenillette, in service with the Bulgarian army, towing a 10.5 cm howitzer in May 1945 in Hungary.

▲ Two T-IV Maybach tanks in service with the Bulgarian army after the First World War.

▼ T-4 Maybach tank, belonging to the training centre, at Poduyane station, Sofia, in November 1945.

▲ The crews of the first T-4 Maybach tanks (Pz.Kpfw. IV Ausf G) delivered by the Germans in May 1943 to the Companies of the 1st and 2nd Battalions.

▼ T-4 Maybach tank, belonging to the Bulgarian Armoured Battalion, as it passes through a Hungarian village during the second phase of the Patriotic War, note the coat of arms with the Bulgarian flag painted diagonally on the schurzen and the skull in white next to the pilot's visor.

THE POST-WAR PERIOD AND THE DISBANDING OF THE BRONIRANA BRIGADA

With the end of the war in May, both the Bronirana Brigade and the 1st Independent Armoured Battalion were withdrawn from the front and returned to Bulgaria, where they would be restructured and reorganised under Soviet supervision.

Before the conflict ended, the Soviets had already proceeded to train an independent armoured regiment in Bulgaria, equipping it with 65 T-34/85 tanks[27]. This supply of tanks, however, was the only one that arrived from May 1945 until the signing of the Paris Peace Treaty of 10 February 1947, in which Bulgaria's entry into the Soviet sphere of influence was sanctioned.

On 1 May 1945, a military parade was held in the capital Sofia in which several armoured units equipped with Škoda tanks also participated.

At the end of 1945, following the reorganisation process of the Bulgarian armoured units, the available means were as follows:

- 15 'Panther' T-V
- 102 Maybach T-IV
- 3 Pz.Kpfw. III
- 56 StuG III
- 11 between StuG IV, Jagdpanzer IV/70(V) and Jagdpanzer IV
- 5 Jagdpanzer 38(t) Hetzer
- 3 Hummel
- 2 Nimrod 40M
- 7 'Prague'
- 23 between Škoda LT-35 and T-11
- 1 Turan
- 19 Renault R35
- 1 SPA
- 8 M-222 and 8 M-223

From this list, as can be seen, there are no T-34/85 tanks, not only the 65 tanks that were supposed to be in service with the Independent Armoured Regiment, but also not the two vehicles provided in early 1945 to begin training.

In 1946, the Bronirana Brigada, also identified as 1st Armoured Brigade, had completed its reorganisation and was equipped with the following tanks:

- 49 between CV33, Škoda LT-35, 'Praga'[28] and R35
- 57 Maybach T-IV Ausf. G, H and J[29]
- 15 Jagdpanzer IV[30]
- 5 StuG III

It is clear that, given the means at its disposal, many of which were obsolete and worn out, the Brigade's function was more of a training nature, in anticipation of receiving Soviet tanks and creating new armoured units.

---

27 According to other sources, the Soviets did not deliver any T-34/85 tanks until 1947 and the Regiment remained in the picture until that date.
28 The 'Praga' tanks remained in service until the early 1950s.
29 In 1955, 11 Maybach T-IVs were still in service in the 1st Armoured Brigade.
30 Most probably, StuG IV and Jagdpanzer IV/70(V) are also included under this single heading, all of which remained in service until the mid-1950s.

The 2nd Armoured Brigade was instead armed with 46 Maybach T-IVs and 56 StuG IIIs.

As of 1 March 1946, 15 Panther T-Vs were in service, 14 of which were operational and 1 under repair. In the spring of 1946, the Soviets delivered a further 6 Panther tanks to the Bulgarians, the last delivery of this vehicle by the Soviets. All Panther T-V tanks were used at the Training School and in the 1st Armoured Brigade in 1945-46.

In 1947, with the establishment of the new Armoured Division, the Bronirana Brigada was officially disbanded and its units were transferred to the new unit. The Armoured Division was formed according to the Soviet order, but already in 1949 it was reorganised into four independent Brigades, each of which was assigned to the Armies of the new Bulgarian People's Army.

The Soviets supplied large quantities of tanks and assault guns to complete the staff of the new Armoured Brigades, vehicles that replaced the German vehicles still in service. By 1950, 466[31] T-34/85 tanks and 156 SU-76M self-propelled vehicles were delivered to Bulgaria.

With the arrival of Soviet assets, German tanks and assault guns, which had survived the conflict, were gradually decommissioned and placed in reserve between 1948 and the early 1950s. As the international situation was still very delicate, and Bulgaria, in the Soviet orbit, bordered Greece and Turkey, nations belonging to NATO, the need arose to strengthen the border defences with these two nations.

Having dozens of Panther T-V[32] and Maybach T-IV tanks in the depots, as well as numerous StuG III assault guns, whose cannons were still more than adequate to fight the adversary's vehicles, a defence system was developed that hinged on fixed positions made up of these vehicles, which in some cases were buried directly in the ground, in other cases only the turret installed on a concrete tank was used, or with part of the vehicle in a concrete tank.

In 1952, the construction of the defensive line, called 'Krali Marko'[33], on the borders with Greece and Turkey began. Seventy German tanks and assault guns were used, remnants of the Second World War: Maybach T-IV, Jagdpanzer IV, StuG III and at least one Panther T-V.

Among the vehicles that were part of the 'Krali Marko', there was an interesting hybrid: the hull of a Maybach T-IV with the turret modified by removing the original 7.5 cm KwK 40 cannon and replacing it with the 76.2 ZiS-3 cannon extrapolated from a self-propelled SU-76M[34].

At the end of the 1990s, the 'Krali Marko' line was abandoned, and the vehicles were left to rust and rot, occasionally used by hunters and hikers as shelter in bad weather. The economic crisis, with the resulting shortage of precious metals, led to an increase in the theft of metal parts from the buried vehicles, owned by the Bulgarian army. Following the theft of an entire Jagdpanzer IV, the army decided to carry out a thorough reconnaissance of the line and found that almost all positions had suffered theft and removal of material.

In 2008, the decision was taken to recover all buried tanks and assault guns, with the intention of reselling them after a cursory restoration, but strong opposition from the veterans' associations blocked the initiative. The following were recovered and restored: 4 Maybach T-IV Ausf. G / H / J, 3 StuG III and one Jagdpanzer L/48, which are now on display at the 'Museum of Battle Glory' in the town of Yambol, while the remaining vehicles were put into storage, awaiting their fate.

With the recovery and restoration of the German tanks and assault guns, the history of these vehicles in the Bulgarian Army came to a definitive end.

---

31   According to other sources, the number of T-34/85 delivered to Bulgaria is 398.
32   The Panther T-V tanks were placed in reserve from 1948, with the prospect of being scrapped in the early 1950s.
33   The name 'Krali Marko' comes from Prince Marko Mrnjavcevic, a pan-Slavic military hero from the 14th century.
34   Only one example of such a tank equipped with this modification was built, although one source mentions two examples being built.

▲ R35 'Reno' tank B60222, belonging to the training centre, about to be loaded onto the railway car at Poduyane station, Sofia, in November 1945.

▼ A tank Pz.Kpfw. V Ausf. G 'Panther' belonging to the training centre at the Poduyane station in Sofia in November 1945.

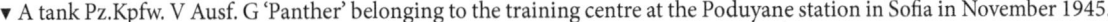

▲ A tank Pz.Kpfw. V Ausf. G 'Panther', followed by a T-4 Maybach, both belonging to the training centre at Poduyane station, Sofia, in November 1945.

▼ One of only two T-34/85s supplied by the Soviets to Bulgaria before the end of the conflict in the spring of 1945.

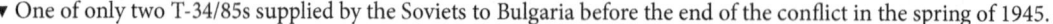

▲ An overview of the vehicles in service at the training centre, taken at the Poduyane station in November 1945, from left: R35, Škoda, Praga, T-4 Maybach, T-5 Panther.

▼ A StuG III buried in the ground belonging to the Krali Marko defence line on the Turkish border in the 1950s.

▲ A T-4 Maybach tank, buried in a concrete tank, belonging to the Krali Marko defence line on the Turkish border in the 1950s.

▼ The recovery of a Jagdpanzer IV, belonging to the 'Krali Marko' line, carried out by the Bulgarian Army after 2008 for restoration.

CAMOUFLAGE, INSIGNIA, REGISTRATION NUMBER

The CV33 'Ansaldo' fast tanks were delivered with the uniform Italian medium green colour scheme, on some tanks dark green spots were painted on the medium green. At the end of the 1930s, all fast tanks were repainted in 3-colour camouflage: dark green, dark yellow and brown, in large spots with sharp edges. In the spring of 1941 they were repainted in uniform dark green.

The Vickers Mk. E tanks arrived from England painted in the original factory 5-colour camouflage, different from the standard camouflage adopted in Bulgaria. As the colouring was of high quality and very durable, it remained so until 1941, when the vehicles began to be repainted in uniform dark green.

The Škoda LT vz.35 and T-11 tanks arrived in Bulgaria painted in uniform panzergrau and remained painted in this colour until the spring of 1944, when the Bulgarian Army, with Service Order No. III-C-132 of 21 January 1944, gave the order to repaint the tanks in dark yellow, but only during extraordinary maintenance or because of the need to repaint the vehicle because the original paint had deteriorated badly. It was also permitted to paint the original panzergrau in dark yellow, but it seems that this opportunity was never used. Some Škoda LT vz.35s were repainted in olive green at the end of hostilities, participating in the 1 May 1945 parade, but most of the surviving tanks remained painted in the original panzergrau colour.

The Renault R35 tanks were delivered painted in uniform panzergrau, in spring 1941 they were repainted in dark green.

When the Pz.Kpfw 38(t) 'Praga' were delivered to Bulgaria, they had already been painted, as required by the Wehrmacht's new directives, in the dark yellow uniform colour given on the original panzergrau. Because of wear and tear, a strange camouflage appeared on many tanks due to the panzergrau colour appearing under the dark yellow. The 'Praga' remained with this colouring until their return to Bulgaria in December 1944. The few tanks still in service in the spring of 1945 were repainted in olive green and participated in the 1 May parade with this colouring.

The Pz.Kpfw. IV tanks were delivered by the Germans painted in uniform dark yellow, with this colour they remained in service until the spring of 1945 when the vehicles intended for operation in the 1st Independent Armoured Battalion were repainted in olive green.

The StuG III assault guns were delivered by the Germans painted in uniform dark yellow with the gun barrel in black, remaining in this colour until their return to Bulgaria at the end of their operational cycle in the Balkans. The vehicles used in combat during 1945 were repainted in olive green.

The M-222 and M-223 armoured cars were delivered from Germany painted in classic panzergrau, the colour in which they ended the war. The vehicles that participated in the parade on 1 May 1945 were repainted in Russian grass green.

The Pz.Kpfw.V 'Panther' tanks were delivered by the Soviets with a uniform colour scheme in classic Russian grass green.

All the various vehicles delivered by the Soviet Union during the course of 1945 in the last months of the war, Pz.Kpfw III, StuH 42, Pz.Kpfw IV, StuG IV, Hummel, StuG III, Jagdpanzer IV, SPA self-propelled vehicles, Nimrod 40M, Turan and Jagdpanzer 38(t) Hetzer, were painted the same colour as the Soviet vehicles in service, Russian grass green.

There is no certain information on the colouring of the SOMUA S35 and Hotchkiss H39 tanks, although, as they were French war prey delivered by the Germans, it is very likely that they were delivered coloured in panzergrau.

In the winter period, a washable white paint was applied to all tanks.

No identifying insignia, nationality or departmental insignia was ever painted on Bulgarian tanks until the declaration of war on Germany in September 1943. Following the entry into the war on the side of the Soviets against the Germans, the *"St. Andrew's Cross"* was painted on tanks and assault guns as a combat insignia in black paint, in some cases also bordered in white, on the sides and rear of the turret, on the front and rear mudguards, on the rear of the hulls next to the plate, on the schürzen in the StuG III, on the schürzen around the turret in the Pz.Kpfw. IV, on the front of the casemate on the 'Praga'. On the Škoda LT vz.35 tanks the *'St. Andrew's Cross'* was painted in white, on the sides of the turret and on the bonnet.

On the StuG III, and in some cases also on the Pz.Kpfw. IV, the *'St. Andrew's Cross'* was painted in black inside a white square.

The only case in which departmental insignia were present was on the M-222 and M-223 armoured cars, where both the front and the back were painted with white paint with the crest of the Reconnaissance Company, a blooming flower reminiscent of a medieval knight's crest, and the crest of the Bronirana Brigada, consisting of four intersecting circles. This coat of arms symbolised the cooperation, in battle, of the four main units serving in the Brigade: the Armoured Regiment, the Motorized Infantry Regiment, the Artillery Regiment and the support units: Engineer, Reconnaissance, Transport, Maintenance, etc.

At the end of the first phase of the Patriotic War, when the units returned to Bulgaria and during the parade in Sofia on 2 December 1944, names of places where battles had been fought against the Germans, or the number of the company they belonged to or of the tank, were painted by the crews on almost all tanks, assault guns and armoured cars. The inscriptions were painted in black or white, while the numbers could be in black or white edged in black.

The 9th Tank Company, equipped with Škoda 'Praga', had its emblem painted on the tanks: a skull with crossed shinbones painted in black on either side of the turret.

When a new Bulgarian armoured unit was sent to fight on the Western Front in early 1945, all *'St Andrew's Crosses'*, place names and various numbers disappeared on the tanks and assault guns, but instead sharp shields with a diagonal Bulgarian tricolour were painted on the sides of the turret and on the rear of the vehicle. In addition, large red stars bordered with a thin white stripe were painted on the front of the vehicle, the sides of the turret and the casemate.

From 17 September 1944, a white rectangle was painted on all vehicles, armoured and armoured vehicles in service with the 2nd Bulgarian Army engaged in fighting in Yugoslavia as an air recognition signal. On trucks, half-tracks and cars it was painted on the front bonnet, on tanks on the turret, right front for the 'Praga' or left bottom for the Škoda, or on the bonnet.

All tanks had a registration number, formed by the letter B (Военен - Army Vehicle) followed by a 5-digit code, where the first 2 indicated the type of vehicle and the remaining 3 the number assigned to the vehicle in ascending order. The registration number, with the letter and digits in black paint and measuring 140 x 70 mm, was written on a white rectangular plate with rounded upper corners, measuring 480 x 170 mm. On StuG IIIs it was painted on the front superstructure, to the right of the gun mantle, and, in rare cases, on the back of the assault cannon centrally above the exhausts, on Pz.Kpfw. IV on the rear of the tank, on the M-222 and M-223 on the front and left rear wing, on the Škoda on the rear in the centre of the plate, on the Vickers a plate was placed on the left rear wing, on the Ansaldo fast tanks on the left rear. The registration number painted on the front of the StuG III casemate was in some cases red.

The registration numbers assigned to the different tanks in service with the Bulgarian armoured forces are as follows:
- CV33/Ansaldo: B60001 to B60014
- Vickers B60015 to B60022
- Škoda LT vz. 35: B60023 to B60048
- Škoda T-11: B60049 to B60058
- Pz.Kpfw 38 (T): B60059 to B60068
- Renault R35: B60201 to B60240
- Pz.Kpfw. IV: B 60250 to B 60337
- StuG III: B60501 to B 60555
- Pz.Kpfw.V: B60415 to B60428 and B60431 to B60436[35]
- M-222 M-223: B 70001 to B 70020

On the sides of the casemate for Ansaldo fast tanks, on the sides of the turret, and in some cases also on the rear, for all other tanks, the last digits of the registration number were painted in large numbers in white paint. For example, if the registration number of a Škoda LT vz. 35 was B 60033, the number 33 was painted on the sides of the turret of the tank.

All tanks that participated in the second phase of the war against Germany in early 1945 no longer had the number painted on the turret, while the registration number on the rear of the vehicle was present and, in the StuG III and Pz.Kpfw. IV, was painted red on a white background.

▲ The skull with crossed shinbones, badge of the 9th Tank Company equipped with 'Praga' tanks.

---

35   These were the last six Panther T-V tanks delivered by the Red Army to Bulgaria in 1946.

▲ The perfectly restored T-4 Maybach (Pz.Kpfw. IV Ausf. H) on display at the National Museum of Military History in Sofia. It represents a vehicle used during the second phase of the Patriotic War in early 1945, painted in dark green and with the Bulgarian flag painted diagonally in the coat of arms on the schurzen.

▼ Škoda tank B60035, with St Andrew's Crosses painted white, parades in Sofia on 2 December 1944.

▲ Photograph of a truck crossing a makeshift bridge in Yugoslavia, one can clearly see the white rectangle painted on the bonnet as an air recognition sign, compulsory on all vehicles during the first phase of the patriotic war.

▼ A Steyr 1500A light truck in service with the Bronirana Brigade during the first phase of the Patriotic War, note the Brigade symbol, the four circles, and the white rectangle on the bonnet as an aerial recognition sign.

BIBLIOGRAPHY

- Ledwoch J., Tank Power N. 116 LT vz. 34-40 TNH, Varsavia, Wydawnictwo Militaria, 2000
- Ledwoch J., Tank Power Vol. XX1 N. 241 - pzKpfw 38(t), Varsavia, Wydawnictwo Militaria, 2006
- Ledwoch J., Tank Power Vol. CLXIV N. 423 - pzKpfw 35(t) LT vz. 35, Varsavia, Wyda. Mil., 2016
- Ledwoch J., Tank Power Vol. N. 325 - Vickers 6-ton Mark E-F vol.II, Varsavia, Wyda. Mil., 2009
- Matev K., Bulgarian Armored Vehicles 1935-1945, Sofia, Angela Publishers, 2000
- http://rotanazdar.cz/?p=2192&lang=cs
- http://ftr.wot-news.com/2013/07/15/bulgarian-armor-part-i/ii/iii/
- https://tanks-encyclopedia.com/ww2/bulgaria/bulgarian-tanks-in-world-war-2
- https://militero.wordpress.com/2010/03/18/bulgarian-tanks-1934-1941/
- https://www.zimmerit.com/zimmeritpedia/BULGARIA_sez_1.html
- www.flamesofwar.com/hobby.aspx?art_id=1021
- https://www.axishistory.com/axis-nations/bulgaria/army/69-bulgaria-army/bulgaria-army-brigades/832-armored-brigade-bulgaria
- https://www.axishistory.com/axis-nations/bulgaria/army/72-bulgaria-army/bulgaria-army-regiments/838-armored-regiment-bulgaria
- https://archive.armorama.com/forums/271468/
- https://it.military-review.com/12534657-armored-vehicles-of-bulgaria-part-1-beginning-1934-1942-biennium
- https://it.military-review.com/12534665-bulgarian-armored-vehicles-part-3-post-war-period-and-modernity
- https://elgrancapitan.org/foro/viewtopic.php?f=68&p=1160727
- https://airgroup2000.com/forum/viewtopic.php?p=5829531
- https://www.armedconflicts.com/vojnovi-i-povojnovi-uzivatelia-t59715
- https://www.armedconflicts.com/vojnovi-i-povojnovi-uzivatelia-t171117
- https://www.valka.cz/Pz-Kpfw-V-Panther-ve-sluzbach-cizich-armad-t40205
- http://it.topwar.ru
- http://tankfront.ru
- https://axisslovakia.tumblr.com/page/23
- https://forums.kitmaker.net/t/bulgarian-wwii-campaign-starts-sep-8th-2021-ends-march-3d-2022/7816/17
- https://www.facebook.com/groups/302283403283940/?locale=eu_ES
- http://www.nabore.bg/statia/kare-oficeri-dokaraha-tankovete-si-na-orlov-most-407-14#%20
- https://wwiiafterwwii.wordpress.com/2021/12/25/the-krali-marko-line/

TITOLI GIÀ PUBBLICATI - TITLES ALREADY PUBLISHING

BOOKS TO COLLECT

www.ingramcontent.com/pod-product-compliance
Lightning Source LLC
LaVergne TN
LVHW081538070526
838199LV00056B/3707